3.8.78

EREX SAGA
and
ÍVENS SAGA

EREX SAGA
AND
ÍVENS SAGA

The Old Norse Versions of
Chrétien de Troyes's Erec *and* Yvain

Translated, with an introduction, by
Foster W. Blaisdell, Jr., and
Marianne E. Kalinke

UNIVERSITY OF NEBRASKA PRESS
Lincoln and London

Publishers on the Plains

UNP

Library of Congress Cataloging in Publication Data

Chrétien de Troyes, 12th cent.
  Erex saga and Ívens saga.

  Includes bibliographical references and index.
  1. Chrétien de Troyes, 12th cent. Chevalier
au lyon. English. 1977. II. Title.
PQ1447.E5B55   841'.1   77–5395
ISBN 0–8032–0925–8

CONTENTS

PREFACE

The tales of King Arthur and his knights not only fascinated medieval audiences throughout Europe but continue to capture the imagination of modern readers. They also continue to influence contemporary literary figures, such as C. S. Lewis, J. R. R. Tolkien, and T. H. White. The medieval Scandinavian branch of the Arthurian literary tradition is, however, relatively unknown to all but the specialists. We hope, therefore, that this translation of *Erex saga* and *Ívens saga* will appeal to a broad readership, and that it may serve to stimulate further interest in Scandinavian Arthurian literature. To that end we have prepared a translation directed toward a general audience and unencumbered by excessive scholarly apparatus.

We wish to express our gratitude to the University Research Committee of the University of Rhode Island for financial support toward the preparation of the manuscript.

FOSTER W. BLAISDELL, JR.
MARIANNE E. KALINKE

INTRODUCTION

The excellent King Arthur ruled over England. . . . He was the most famous of all those kings who have ruled on this side of the ocean and the most popular after Charlemagne. He had the bravest knights in all Christendom.

1.

The opening words of *Ívens saga* might have struck a responsive chord in the hearts of many listeners in the Middle Ages, for stories of King Arthur and the Knights of the Round Table were great favorites and circulated widely throughout Europe. Although he was not the creator of the Arthurian legend, Chrétien de Troyes deserves credit for raising the "matter of Britain" to literary eminence. His various romances quickly engendered translations, adaptations, and imitations throughout Europe. *Erex saga* and *Ívens saga*, the two sagas translated in this volume, have as their main source Chrétien's *Erec et Enide* (ca. 1170) and *Yvain* (ca. 1177–81), as do the Middle High German *Erec* (ca. 1190) and *Iwein* (ca. 1202) by Hartmann von Aue, the Middle English *Ywain and Gawain* (ca. 1350), and the Swedish *Ivan Lejonriddaren* (1303).[1]

Probably the least known and most neglected adaptations of Chrétien de Troyes's *Erec et Enide* and *Yvain* are the Scandinavian *riddarasögur* (tales of chivalry) *Erex saga* and *Ívens saga*. Until recently the existence of a Scandinavian Arthurian literature was recognized by only a handful of specialists.[2] Partly to blame for this is the excellence the native Scandinavian literature which flourished in the thirteenth century—the great age of saga-writing coincided with the

introduction of continental romances to the North. Since the
riddarasögur are derivative and have been considered inferior
to the native literature by some scholars, it is understandable
that they would not especially interest most Scandinavianists.
Arthurians too have largely ignored the Scandinavian
branch of the Arthurian literary tradition. In such a standard
reference work as Roger Sherman Loomis's *The Development of
Arthurian Romance* no reference is made to the Arthurian
riddarasögur, in spite of the fact that this eminent medievalist
had "endeavoured to write a history of Arthurian literature in
the Middle Ages."[3] Lack of interest in these *riddarasögur* can
be ascribed to a large extent to a certain linguistic inacces-
sibility of the material, whether primary or secondary, most of
which is in one or another of the Scandinavian languages.
Another factor may be the mistaken notion of many that these
works are nothing but summaries of French originals.

Some scholars might justify ignoring the Scandinavian
Arthurian literature by pointing out that the northern re-
dactors failed to understand some of the essential qualities of
the French sources. Others might criticize the Scandinavian
redactors for casting metrical romances, highly lyric at times,
into paratactic prose narratives more suited to conveying
everyday reality than the Arthurian world of love, adventure,
and fantasy. However, *Erex saga* and *Ívens saga* are more than
just abridged translations; they are interpretations of the
French works. The various omissions and changes of source
material are to be attributed not so much to a misunder-
standing of the original as to an intentional transformation
designed to produce a work adhering to native literary con-
ventions and expressing the redactor's personal style and
sense of structure, as is especially clear in *Erex saga*.

        2.

        Unlike the German and English derivatives of
Chrétien's *Erec* and *Yvain*, which are rhymed metrical ro-
mances, the Scandinavian redactions are prose narratives—like
the indigenous Icelandic sagas. Moreover, the repetitive, sub-
jective, and at times psychoanalytical approach of Chrétien de

Troyes is transformed into the terse, impersonal style favored by the native literary tradition of the thirteenth century.

Erex saga is more extreme than *Ívens saga* in paring down the French text; it is succinct to the point of being laconic— and that in spite of two interpolated adventures which are independent additions to the Scandinavian version. One is hard put to find one superfluous word in *Erex saga*. In this respect *Ívens saga* differs; the redactor was more faithful to his source. He retained many repetitive elements, even adding some of his own, which he frequently chose to express in alliterative formulae.

Alliteration is often mentioned as a stylistic characteristic of the *riddarasögur* and its use is sometimes assumed to be indiscriminate.[4] *Erex saga* and *Ívens saga* seem to hold a unique position: except for a few isolated occurrences of alliteration, so isolated in fact that one is tempted to consider them coincidence, this stylistic device is not found in *Erex saga*; in *Ívens saga*, on the other hand, alliteration occurs frequently, but not indiscriminately, for it is found primarily in passages of dramatic intensity.

Generally the alliterative patterns in *Ívens saga* occur at high points of the narrative and are sometimes sustained through several clauses as, for example, in Íven's first visit to the spring (p. 44) and when Íven mourns the loss of his wife's affection (p. 65). In such passages the shortcomings of our translation are most apparent, for many of the alliterative patterns had to be sacrificed for the sake of accuracy of meaning.

Of the two sagas *Erex saga* departs more radically from the French source by substantially reordering the sequence of events according to what seems to have been a preconceived symmetrical structure. Through the omission or rearrangement of certain of Chrétien's material, as well as through the interpolation of two new episodes, the Scandinavian redactor created a new structure for this tale.[5] He moved the description of the hero, who does not appear until line 83 of the romance, to the very beginning of the saga. In so doing, he followed the native literary tradition, which frequently portrays the protagonist before the action unfolds. To the end of the saga the redactor appended what may be called an epilogue—again standard literary practice in the sagas—to give information about Erex's rule and descendants. The redactor completely revised the structure of the French tale by rearranging and combining existing narrative units and by creating two new episodes. Erex encounters Kay at the very end of his journey of adventure (p. 27), just prior to the "Joy of the Court" episode, whereas in the French romance this incident occurs after the duel with Guivrez (the Scandinavian Guimar, p. 20).[6] In the French source Erec has to fight first against three robbers and immediately afterwards against five armed knights, but the saga redactor combined these into one adventure involving eight robbers (p. 16–17). Then the redactor also interpolated two entirely new episodes in chapter 10, one with a flying dragon, another with seven armed men, which are admirably integrated in content and style into the whole.[7] Moreover, these new episodes are an intrinsic part of a carefully balanced structure of parallel and contrasting pairs.

The authorial presence of the Scandinavian redactors is evident throughout both sagas. The saga author's literary heritage manifests itself in the formulaic openings of several chapters of *Erex saga* (chaps. 1, 3, 5, 10, 11, 12) and once in *Ívens saga* (chap. 8). The redactor at times steps forward to give explanations, as when he clarifies the meaning of the loan word *Pentecost* in the opening chapter of *Ívens saga*. Where names are concerned divergent forms can in many cases be attributed to poor copying, but frequently the redactors, especially the author of *Erex saga*, seem to have given their imagination free rein as they substituted for the French forms or added names where the original provided none. For example, the name of the knight held captive by the two giants is Cadoc of Tabriol in Chrétien's *Erec* (1. 4515), whereas in the saga he is called Kalviel of Karinlisborg; moreover, the knight's lady, who is nameless in the romance, receives a name as well as a father in the saga (p. 22).

In *Erex saga* one suspects a cleric at work because of the addition of a number of didactic comments with religious overtones as, for example, in chapter 4 the queen's statement to Malpirant on the need to control one's anger (p. 10), or in chapter 11, the refusal of the retainers of Earl Placidus to sanction his marriage to Evida without her consent (p. 26). Minor yet telling additions also point to the redactor's cultural heritage. In response to Kalebrant's inquiry as to the identity of the wild man in chapter 2 of *Ívens saga*, the knight hears: "I never change my shape" (p. 39). The reference, not found in the French *Yvain*, is probably to a person, found in Old Norse literature, who was capable of assuming the form of various animals (cf. Old Icelandic *hamramr*). In the same saga, chapter 12, Íven protests to the accusers of Luneta that he did not bring the lion to fight against them like a *berserkr* (p. 70), i.e., one of the wild warriors found in the sagas who fought as though possessed by frenzy.[8]

One of the major problems facing the Scandinavian redactors who translated the Arthurian romances was their "courtliness." The chivalric code, especially as it was expressed in service to ladies, was alien to the Scandinavian culture, and the redactors of *Erex saga* and *Ívens saga* frequently made considerable changes, especially in characterization, which in turn influenced the plot, and thus the very tenor of the story.

In chapter 5 the redactor of *Erex saga* has King Arthur explain why he kisses Evida (p. 12). Chrétien's King Arthur, however, declares his love for Enide, and calls her his sweet friend (11. 1837–40),[9] but such an expression of "courtly" love needed to be explained to the northern audience; the redactor thus precludes the possibility of criticism or misunderstanding by those not familiar with courtly manners and ritual.

To make the "Joy of the Court" episode more acceptable to his audience, the redactor of *Erex saga* had to make some additions. The absolute enslavement of a knight in service to his lady, which is depicted in the romance (11. 6090 ff.), must not have been acceptable to the saga redactor and thus he provided an explanation for this strange behavior: the lady is the daughter of a powerful earl, but her lover is only a knight. By withdrawing to a secluded spot she had hoped that her father would not discover their whereabouts. Thus, the romantic notion of the knight enslaved by his beloved was transformed into the more realistic dilemma of inequality of social standing. Marriage with a man of inferior rank brought with it loss of honor, something a Scandinavian audience could well understand.

Chapter 3 of *Erex saga* departs drastically from the source in depicting the first meeting of Erex and Evida. In the romance the hero's primary concern is the knight whose ugly dwarf has struck the queen's lady in waiting, and he bargains with Enide's father for arms. He proposes to enter the contest for the sparrow hawk on behalf of Enide. *If he succeeds* he will take her with him and crown her his queen (11. 659 ff.). The proposal is contingent, however, on the father supplying Erec with arms. Thus, Erec sees Enide at first solely as a means to an end—getting arms in order to avenge himself. The father agrees to this bargain without consulting his daughter. In the saga, however, Erex proposes before he even learns about the contest; Erex's subsequent marriage is thus only coincidentally associated with his encounter with Malpirant. Moreover, the father agrees to the marriage only if his daughter raises no objections.

This occurrence of deference to a woman's wishes is not an isolated instance; in chapter 11 of *Erex saga*, Earl Placidus does *not* marry Evida—in the romance, the wedding ceremony actually takes place—because she refuses to grant her consent. In *Ívens saga* the hero is offered a beautiful maiden, by her father no less, as reward for battling against two giants (p. 75). The saga redactor is willing to incorporate this incident from the romance but makes a change; whereas the French Yvain chivalrously points out that only the emperor of Germany could be deserving of her beauty (11. 5482 ff.), the Scandinavian is horrified at the suggestion of bargaining for a woman and expresses his distaste.

The romance's attitude toward woman, who is at the same time an object of slavelike veneration and a piece of property to be acquired and disposed of at will, gives way to the image of the rather independent woman found frequently in the native sagas. Although there are instances in the indigenous Scandinavian literature of marriage contracts made without consulting the opinion of the woman involved, there are also sufficient examples which indicate that a woman did have a say concerning her fate and that she resented or balked at decisions made for her by male relatives. Especially the fact that the retainers of Earl Placidus respect Evida's wishes indicates native influence. As far as the earl and his retainers are concerned, Evida is a widow, and hence, according to Scandinavian law, had more of a right to decide for herself whether she would remarry and to choose her own husband.[10]

Not only in depicting the attitudes and behavior of men towards women did the redactors of *Erex saga* and *Ívens saga* make changes but also in dealing with a man's honor and reputation. The redactor of *Erex saga* clearly identifies honor as the driving force in Erex's behavior.[11] His response to Evida's criticism of his manner of life (p. 15) indicates that he considers her his equal and that his sole reason for undertaking the journey is to remove any further cause for reproach and to restore his honor. The saga author seems to have interpreted Evida's criticism in the spirit of the native sagas, where not infrequently it is a function of a woman to egg a man on to action.

Erex's response to criticism of his life of ease is quite different from that of Erec in the French work; the adventures that follow Erec's *recreantise*, while intended to restore Erec's lost honor, also seem meant to test Enide's fidelity and to punish her for daring to criticize her husband for his sloth.[12] This latter motivation is lacking in the saga; with the exception of two instances of reproach, which are insufficiently motivated and seem to have been inadvertently retained from the romance, Erex is a most considerate husband at all times. He sets out neither to test nor to punish his wife; his sole motive is to restore his lost honor.

This change of motivation for Erex's behavior is part of a pattern in *Erex saga* and *Ívens saga*. In both works knights become guilty of dishonorable behavior, but, unlike their French counterparts, they consistently admit to it. The French Erec who is whipped by the dwarf pleads for understanding for his cowardly retreat (11. 238 ff.), whereas the Scandinavian Erex confesses outright that he is disgraced for not having dared to avenge himself (p. 5). In *Yvain* Calogrenant

tells about his disgraceful episode at the fountain only with
the greatest reluctance, and only after having been asked to
do so several times. He considers himself foolish for telling his
tale of shame (11. 579 ff.). The Scandinavian Kalebrant, on
the other hand, also confesses to foolishness, but in his dis-
honorable conduct rather than in telling his story (p. 42).
When the French Yvain realizes that he has broken his pledge
to Laudine, he bemoans the loss of his comfort and joy (1.
3542), but Íven adds loss of honor and reputation to his
catalogue of misfortunes (p. 65).

Finally, there are some additions and changes in the sagas
which are the results neither of the redactors' stylistic idio-
syncrasies nor of cultural assimilation. The sudden appear-
ance of Íven's female companion in chapter 13 of *Ívens saga* is
such an example. Since she comes on the scene after a lacuna
in the Icelandic manuscript, the explanation must be sought
in the French text, according to which she is a friend of the
younger daughter of the lord of Noire Espine (11. 4703 ff.),
after whose death the older daughter claims the total in-
heritance. The latter persuades Gawain to champion her
cause. When the younger daughter seeks help at Arthur's
court, there is no one there who is willing to aid her, but she
is given forty days in which to secure a champion (1. 4803).
She learns of Yvain, the Knight of the Lion, and proceeds to
search for him, but when she gets ill, another girl, the friend
mentioned above, takes up the search in her stead (11.
4832–34). In the French text it is this other girl who finds
Yvain and is present for the adventure that follows (11.
5109 ff.). In the saga, however, the girl accompanying Íven is
the daughter herself. It thus seems that in the complete
version of *Ívens saga* the redactor had fused the figures of the
two girls, so that only the daughter is searching for Íven; it is
she who finds him and conducts him to Arthur's court. This
may be the same kind of change that we find in *Erex saga*,
where two separate groups of robbers are combined into one
by the Norse redactor, as already mentioned. Moreover, the
redactor made another change for which we see no obvious
explanation: the reversal of roles of the two sisters. It is the
younger daughter who claims the total inheritance in the saga,

not the older girl as in the French romance; thus, the girl who suddenly appears in Íven's company and who has been cheated by her sister is the older daughter.

Erex saga and *Ívens saga* unfortunately and inaccurately have become known as condensed "translations" of Chrétien de Troyes's romances; the term *translation* is inaccurate because these two sagas, especially *Erex saga*, are as much adaptations of the French romances as are Hartmann von Aue's *Erec* and *Iwein*. Although these two *riddarasögur* may be stylistically inferior to their German counterparts and to their French sources, they should not be dismissed lightly. Of the works based on Chrétien de Troyes's *Erec et Enide* and *Yvain*, *Erex saga* and *Ívens saga* are the only instances of material adapted to a culture that was as yet unfamiliar with the courtly civilization of continental Europe and England. *Erex saga* and *Ívens saga* are examples of "translating" one literary genre, the rhymed metrical romance, into another, the prose saga; they are also striking instances of adapting material basic to one culture to the needs of an audience rooted in a rather different culture.

3.

The concluding lines of *Ívens saga* tell us that the translation was prepared for King Hákon the Old. This is the Norwegian king Hákon Hákonarson who had the Thomas version of the Tristan material translated in 1226.[13] We may view the translation of *Ívens saga*, then, as another block in a plan of the king which would ultimately introduce into medieval Scandinavia some of the finest works of Continental culture. Part of the intent was, no doubt, to provide the king's court with entertainment, but there were additional benefits to be gained. The introduction of more "courtly" European culture, in whatever aspect, could only strengthen the position of the king at home and might possibly also elevate the reputation of his country abroad.[14] Thus, *Ívens saga* possesses some significance not only for the literary history of Scandinavia, and even of medieval Europe in general, but also for cultural and political developments of the time. Although for

Ívens saga there is no indication of the precise date of the original translation in any preserved manuscript, it is logical to place the work in close conjunction with *Tristrams saga*, a translation of Thomas's *Tristan*.

Exactly when and how *Ívens saga* reached Iceland we do not know, but the fact remains that all extant manuscripts of the saga are Icelandic; no Norwegian manuscripts are preserved. And the same applies to *Erex saga*, as well as to *Tristrams saga*. In Iceland these new works obviously took hold and flourished. They were copied and recopied and even came to exert a certain influence on native Icelandic productions.[15] From Norway the influence of *Ívens saga* also spread eastward into Sweden. There we find a version in verse (rhyming couplets), one of the so-called *Eufemiavisor*. *Ivan Lejonriddaren* ("Ivan, the Knight of the Lion") was translated in 1303 from French, according to a statement in the text, for the Norwegian queen Eufemia. Investigation of the work suggests, however, that the translator used in addition to a French text a copy of the Norwegian prose translation. But why into Swedish? Again, the answer is to some extent political. In 1302 Duke Erik Magnusson of Sweden visited the Norwegian court, one purpose of the visit being the arrangement of his engagement to Princess Ingeborg, the daughter of Eufemia.[16] The Swedish translation, consequently, appears to have been intended as a sort of "good-will gesture."

Concerning the place and date for the translation of *Erex saga* we know very little, unfortunately. There is no statement in its text as now preserved comparable to the one at the conclusion of *Ívens saga*, and it seems unlikely that the original translation ever contained such a statement. Several of the manuscripts which happen to contain both sagas show the concluding lines of *Ívens saga*. We would reason that one and the same scribe would probably not have copied the statement in one saga but have deleted a similar passage in the other. In spite of the lack of any direct textual reference, we think it only logical to set the acquisition of a manuscript of Chrétien's *Erec* and the translation of *Erex saga* in conjunction with that of *Ívens saga*, as well as with the other activities of a similar nature referred to above.

4.

Neither *Erex saga* nor *Ívens saga* is preserved in an original manuscript; all are later copies. For *Ívens saga* we have two fifteenth-century vellums, Stockholm 6 4to and AM 489 4to, while the third primary text is a seventeenth-century paper manuscript, Stockholm 46 fol. For *Erex saga* the primary manuscripts are two seventeenth-century paper ones, AM 18lb fol. and Stockholm 46 (again). There are also two small vellum fragments from about 1500, but they preserve only some eight lines of text. For both sagas there are also a number of paper copies from the seventeenth century and later.

Both vellums of *Ívens saga* are defective. Stockholm 6 has two lacunae of probably one leaf each, the first at page 45 after "it came so close" through page 48, "saw him musing" in our translation, and the other at page 73 after "and great hospitality" through page 73, "a quick death tomorrow." Approximately the last third of AM 489 is now missing, from page 69, "his sons and daughter" on, and a number of the preserved leaves are badly damaged in spots. This damage causes particular difficulty where we are unable to refer to the text of Stockholm 6, that is, at the first lacuna. We have then had to rely on a later paper copy of AM 489. Stockholm 46 is complete and in good condition, but it presents a much shortened version of the saga, by roughly two-fifths. For the first lacuna in Stockholm 6 we have, of course, the text of AM 489 (or of its copy), but the second lacuna comes after the end of that manuscript. We must therefore rely on the text of Stockholm 46, even though it is considerably shortened and seems defective in other respects. This situation concerning the manuscripts explains why there are certain difficulties with the text, and consequently with our translation, for example in the matter of the girl who suddenly appears in Íven's company in chapter 13. At least part of Chrétien's story which is missing here would presumably have been contained in the lost portions of the two vellums, but the text of Stockholm 46 never explains the girl, although it does supply some of Chrétien's missing details. We have tried to make the translation here as coherent as possible but did not wish to depart any more than absolutely necessary from the preserved text.

The two primary manuscripts of _Erex saga_ are complete and in relatively good condition, even though they are later and therefore conceivably subject to more change in the process of copying. Naturally, just how many "generations" of copies lie between the original translation and the manuscripts we have today we have no way of knowing. We also do not know when chapter 10, the interpolation, was added, but the text of that chapter, as we have pointed out in section 2, is well integrated into the saga as it now exists.

Erex saga has been edited twice, by the Swedish scholar Gustaf Cederschiöld in 1880 (Copenhagen, vol. 3 in the series Samfund til udgivelse af gammel nordisk litteratur), and in 1965 by Foster Blaisdell (Copenhagen; in Editiones Arnamagnæanæ, series B, vol. 19). The latter edition prints a diplomatic text of both primary manuscripts (followed by a very close literal translation designed solely as a control for the unnormalized text). There is also a popular edition, based on Cederschiöld, edited by Valdimar Ásmundarson in 1886 (Reykjavik; in _Ævintýrasögur_ vol. 2). _Ivens saga_ was edited twice by the German scholar Eugen Kölbing, in 1872 (Strassburg; in _Riddarasögur_) and in 1898 (Halle; in Altnordische Saga-Bibliothek, vol. 7). Kölbing provided notes of comparison not only with the French original but also with the medieval Swedish, English, and German versions. Bjarni Vilhjálmsson also published a popular edition, in modern Icelandic, based on Kölbing, in 1954 (Reykjavik; in _Riddarasögur_, vol. 2). A diplomatic edition is being prepared by Foster Blaisdell.

We have based our translation on the diplomatic edition (1965) for _Erex saga_ and the manuscript materials available to Blaisdell for _Ivens saga_. Our translation represents in some respects a conflation of the primary manuscripts (respectively two and three), with Chrétien's text as our "guide." That is, when the manuscripts showed different readings, we selected the one which was the closest to the French. We reason that, since the sagas are translations of the two medieval French works, the readings closest to these would probably represent the original ones. At the same time, when the saga manuscripts agree, we altered nothing in order to conform to the French. For example, the roles of the two sisters in chapters 14–15 of *Ívens saga* are reversed, as compared with what Chrétien has, but our translation follows the text of the saga. We have also tried to be faithful to the style of these sagas, while recognizing that this is a difficult, delicate matter. The sagas have a very characteristic style, certain features of which we have tried to reproduce. Others we decided had to be dropped. One striking feature is the use of alliterative pairs in *Ívens saga*, and this we have tried to retain wherever possible, e.g., "*a*rmed in full *a*rmor" (p. 38), "a *l*ady so *l*ovely" (p. 47). There are also certain formulae which occur at the beginning of chapters; this is a feature found in other sagas as well. Without being absolutely literal, we have nevertheless tried to retain some of the formulaic nature of these openings, e.g., in *Erex saga* at chapters 5, 10, 11. Another striking feature of the style is a frequent shift from the past tense to the present in narration, even within the same sentence. This we have not tried to reproduce. Throughout both sagas there is a certain uniformity of tone, a certain formality, even in the dialogue. We wanted to try to give something of this "flavor" but have tried to avoid a too monotonous tone. We are probably most free in some of the direct speech. The frequent use of such adverbs as *now, then, there* is also a characteristic of the style of these sagas, and again we have tried to retain the flavor, though by no means all occurrences. Finally, certain passages in both sagas are simply obscure, or ambiguous. Some of these we have interpreted to the best of our ability, but others we have left as is.

Both in this Introduction and in our Notes to the Translation we have tried to limit our references—in the "spirit" of the translation—to works in English which ought to be more or less readily available. There is obviously a great deal of relevant scholarship which we have thus ignored.

Notes to the Introduction

1. The Welsh *Gereint* and *Owein* are counterparts to Chrétien's *Erec* and *Yvain*, but the relationship between the French and Welsh romances is not clear. Scholars today generally think that the Welsh versions do not derive from Chrétien de Troyes, but that they are adaptations of the same sources as Chrétien must have used. For a full discussion of the Arthurian tradition, see Roger Sherman Loomis, ed., *Arthurian Literature in the Middle Ages* (Oxford: Clarendon Press, 1959), especially the following chapters: chap. 6, on the diffusion of the Arthurian legend on the European continent; chap. 15, on Chrétien de Troyes; chap. 16, for *Gereint* and *Owein*; chap. 33, for Hartmann's *Erec* and *Iwein*; chap. 37, for the Middle English *Ywain and Gawain*.

2. See P. M. Mitchell, "Scandinavian Literature," chap. 35 of Loomis, ed., *Arthurian Literature*, for a discussion of the Arthurian material in Scandinavia; also, Margaret Schlauch, *Romance in Iceland* (Princeton and New York: Princeton University Press and American-Scandinavian Foundation, 1934).

3. Roger Sherman Loomis, *The Development of Arthurian Romance* (London: Hutchinson, 1963), p. 7.

4. For a discussion of this stylistic device, see Paul Schach, "Style and Structure of *Tristrams Saga*," in *Scandinavian Studies: Essays Presented to Dr. Henry Goddard Leach on the Occasion of His Eighty-fifth Birthday*, ed. Carl F. Bayerschmidt and Erik J. Friis (Seattle: University of Washington Press for the American-Scandinavian Foundation, 1965), pp. 71–73.

5. See Sister Jane A. Kalinke, "The Structure of the *Erex Saga*," *Scandinavian Studies* 42 (1970): 343–55.

6. Concerning the forms of the various names we observe the following conventions. We use the Old Norse forms, e.g., Erex, Evida, and Íven, when referring to the sagas and in the translation itself, but the French forms, e.g., Erec, Enide, and Yvain, when referring to Chrétien's works. Although Erex, for example, ultimately derives from Erec, Erex within the context of the saga is really a very different "person." In the case of a few names which occur especially frequently in most works of Arthurian literature and with which many of our readers will already be familiar, e.g., Arthur,

Gawain, and Kay, we have used the common (English) form rather than the Old Norse (as, Gawain for Valven). In addition, these forms vary not only from saga to saga but also from manuscript to manuscript of the same saga.

7. For a detailed discussion of the parallelism between the interpolated material and other parts of the saga, see Foster W. Blaisdell, "The Composition of the Interpolated Chapter in the *Erex Saga,*" *Scandinavian Studies* 36 (1964): 118–26.

8. See, for example, Peter G. Foote and David M. Wilson, *The Viking Achievement* (New York: Praeger, 1970), p. 285.

9. References to Chrétien de Troyes are to reprints (Amsterdam: Rodopi, 1965) of the critical editions of Wendelin Foerster, *Christian von Troyes sämtliche Werke*, vol. 2, *Der Löwenritter* (Halle: Max Niemeyer, 1887); vol. 3, *Erec und Enide* (Halle: Max Niemeyer, 1890).

10. See, for example, Foote and Wilson, *Viking Achievement*, p. 110.

11. See Marianne E. Kalinke, "Honor: The Motivating Principle of the *Erex Saga,*" *Scandinavian Studies* 45 (1973): 135–43.

12. Romance scholars do not agree concerning Erec's motivation in setting out on adventure. For a review of the various scholarly opinions, see Kalinke, "Honor: The Motivating Principle of the *Erex Saga,*" especially pp. 135–37.

13. *The Saga of Tristram and Ísönd*, trans. Paul Schach (Lincoln: University of Nebraska Press, 1973); see especially p. xvii.

14. For a general treatment of the situation, see Henry Goddard Leach, *Angevin Britain and Scandinavia* (Cambridge: Harvard University Press, 1921).

15. See, for example, Peter Hallberg, *The Icelandic Saga*, trans. Paul Schach (Lincoln: University of Nebraska Press, 1962), pp. 142 ff.

16. Alrik Gustafson, *A History of Swedish Literature* (Minneapolis: University of Minnesota Press, 1961), pp. 34–35.

EREX
SAGA

Add. Ms. 38117, f. 193. King Arthur hunting a stag. Reproduced by permission of the British Library Board.

This story opens as King Arthur was holding court in his castle which was called Kardigan. It was the Easter season and he was maintaining his court as magnificently as had always been his custom; no one could remember ever having seen such royal splendor elsewhere.

On his daily rides and at his round table Arthur had the company of his twelve wise men and counselors. One of these, the son of King Ilax, was outstanding in chivalrous deeds. He was handsome in appearance, a most accomplished man, and not over twenty-five years of age when this story took place. His name was Erex. He was highly esteemed not only by the king and queen but also by all the courtiers.

One could now see assembled there many a good knight, as well as kings and earls and other worthy men, both young and old, and well-versed in chivalrous behavior. They were eager to show off their prowess, not only to other noble men but also to the well-bred young ladies in the queen's retinue, who came from good families. There were very few maidens who had not chosen for themselves a sweetheart. For those who desired it there was no lack of entertainment either to be seen or heard. Everyone was either busy chatting with his sweetheart or engaged in some other form of entertainment of his choice; all were gracious and well-disposed towards one another.

And when all were in high spirits, the king called for silence and then spoke: "It is well-known to you that here in this forest there roams a certain hart which we have never been able to hunt down. Now whoever succeeds in bagging it shall be rewarded with a kiss from the most beautiful maiden in my court. Therefore, let all those who intend to accompany me to the hunt be ready early tomorrow morning."

Gawain, an excellent knight and nephew of the king, responded to Arthur's speech. "My Lord," he said, "this expedition may result in great difficulties, for each one of us would rather fight than let another man's sweetheart be pronounced more beautiful than his own."

At these words the king became angry and declared: "Whether you like it or not, Gawain, we shall nevertheless proceed as I have indicated, for no vassal has the right to refuse to carry out what his lord has commanded."

CHAPTER 2

Early in the morning the king, accompanied by his retainers, rode to the forest. Each one now pursued the hart as best he could. Some shouted, some blew their trumpets, still others urged on the hunting and herd dogs so that there was a great din because of the neighing horses and baying hounds. Ahead of them all rode King Arthur on a strong charger, swift as a swallow in flight.

The queen also rode into the forest with her retinue and accompanied by young Erex who was mounted on a fine steed which had come from Spain. He wore a mantle of red silk, a tunic fashioned from a precious white cloth, and silken hose. The horse's bridle bit was of silver, the saddle carved from ivory, and the spurs of pure gold.

So swiftly did the queen ride into the forest that no one was able to follow her but Erex and a young lady in waiting, the daughter of a king. They came to a halt in a clearing quite removed from the rest of the party. Except for a sword Erex was unarmed. They dismounted to allow their horses to rest. Thereupon they caught sight of a fully armed knight riding forth out of the forest; he was accompanied by a beautiful maiden. Before them rode an ugly dwarf on a large stallion; he carried in his hand an ell-long horsewhip.

The queen now turned to her lady in waiting and said: "Ride quickly and bid that knight come to me, for I would like to find out who he is."

The maiden rode off speedily and approached the dwarf,

who addressed her. "Fair maiden," said he, "tell me whom you are seeking."

The girl answered: "The queen sent me to find out who this knight is and to ask him to approach her."

To this the dwarf responded: "Turn back at once, for you will not get past me."

"Good dwarf," the maiden said, "let me proceed so that I can carry out my errand."

The dwarf in turn became angry and struck such a blow with his whip that her hand was spattered with blood.

Thereupon she turned back weeping to report to the queen, who declared: "It is obvious that this knight is discourteous since he allows to go unavenged his dwarf's dastardly behavior, which has brought such disgrace upon a girl. You, Erex, my good knight, ride forward and find out the identity of this knight."

Erex now charged to the spot where the dwarf was. The latter called out to him: "Turn back you fool, for you won't get past me."

Erex replied: "Creep off, you loathsome creature; I'll continue on my errand whether you like it or not," and shoved him aside.

"No, no," protested the dwarf, "I'm not afraid of you, for my master will avenge me at once if you do me harm." At that he raised the whip with both hands and lashed at Erex's neck with such force that he flayed the skin off and Erex all but fainted. Erex was now both distressed and angry, yet he did not avenge himself on the spot because he did not trust himself to fight unarmed against a stranger who was fully armed.

Under these circumstances he turned back and told the queen what had occurred and that a double disgrace had befallen him—"but it is especially terrible that I did not dare avenge myself. However, this I swear to you, my queen, that I shall not return to King Arthur's court until I have avenged both your dishonor and mine—or get another far greater. I shall now pursue them swiftly. May God grant you joy."

The queen thanked him for his words, and when they parted, she and the maiden wished him luck more than a hundred times over.

Erex rode off now, but the queen stayed behind in the forest until the king, who had hunted down the hart, arrived with his men. They now rode back to the castle where they proceeded to table.

When all were in high spirits, the king started to speak: "I would now like to collect from the most beautiful young lady present that kiss which I have earned with my spear."

At this request there arose such discord that all the retainers nearly came to blows, because each one considered his sweetheart to be the most beautiful one. When the situation had reached such a dangerous point, the queen asked to be heard and her request was granted. She now informed King Arthur of the events which had occurred in the forest and which had led to Erex's departure, and she asked him to delay the kiss until they had received news from Erex. He consented gladly, as did all the retainers.

CHAPTER 3

Now Erex, as was already told earlier, followed the knight until evening, when they came to a strong and large castle. There were many people there and great mirth, but as soon as they saw the armed knight, their merriment ceased. They followed the knight to his lodgings, and it seemed as though no one saw Erex.

Erex rode on now until he came to a spot where an old man was sitting on the steps of a castle, handsome in appearance, yet poorly dressed and rather woebegone. He bade Erex be welcome, and the old man's invitation was gladly accepted. Erex dismounted and the master of the house called to his daughter to lead away the horse.

The girl was in a worn and tattered linen dress, yet her whole body was so lovely that Erex thought he had never seen the like. Moreover, she had such bearing and such fine manners that Nature herself marveled that she was so lovely in form. Erex immediately fell head over heels in love with her. When she saw Erex, she too fell in love with him, although it seemed strange to her that she should be able to love a stranger. They now stood and looked at each other, and when the host saw this, he proceeded to lead Erex's horse to a stall where he gave it grain and beer. But the maiden waited on Erex and led him to a seat where they passed the time in friendly conversation.

When the master of the house came in, Erex greeted him in a most friendly way and addressed him: "Your daughter is the most beautiful girl in all the world, yet I wonder why she is so poorly clothed. But to come right to the point, it is my desire and request that you give this young lady to me in marriage, because I love her more than all my father's gold and kingdom. It will only further your honor, if I am allowed to marry her. I have no intention of concealing my name from you—I am Erex, the son of King Ilax and I have been with King Arthur for five years. With this young lady I wish both to live and to die. I now leave the decision in your hands."

The master of the house was now very glad when he found out about Erex's family, and said: "I have often heard people speak about your bravery and chivalrous deeds, and by no means do I wish to refuse to give you my daughter in marriage—if that is her wish. She is not so poorly clothed because she was born in thralldom—indeed, Earl Melan is her mother's brother—but I have been at war for such a long time, that I have lost both my possessions and my patrimony. Formerly I was powerful and had great authority among the chieftains, but now no one considers me worth anything since poverty overtook me. Nevertheless, I suspect that my daughter possesses no less intelligence and womanly skills than beauty. Now let her speak her own mind."

Her answer was not hard to obtain, and the betrothal now took place. Thereafter they went to table and were cheerful and in good spirits. They had one cook to prepare the meal, but no other servants.

Erex now inquired who that knight was who had ridden in the evening into the castle with a lady and accompanied by a dwarf, and from where those people came who were amusing themselves there.

The master of the house replied: "That knight is called Malpirant and he is an outstanding champion and an accomplished man. He has overcome many a good knight. Every year he arranges a certain competition, which is to take place once more tomorrow. The nature of this event is as follows: This knight has a sparrow hawk made of gold, which is attached to a pole six ells long and made of silver. He will erect this pole in a certain field. The knight has a beautiful sweetheart, but should there be any knight so bold as to wish to carry off the pole on behalf of his own lady, and to claim that sparrow hawk for himself, then that knight must ride in the tournament and fight with Malpirant. Both life and possessions are at stake for the one who is defeated."

Erex now told him what had brought him on this journey and what he had to repay the knight.

"I see," said the master of the house. "I would like to provide you with such good weapons and such a good horse for this combat that you can't find any better in this country."

Erex thanked him for his kindness. Then they went to bed. Erex was little worried about his affairs.

Early next morning Erex rose and went to church where he had the Mass of the Holy Spirit said. Evida, his sweetheart, had also come, and they commended themselves to God. After the morning drink he armed himself and mounted his horse without supporting himself with either stirrup or saddle bow. His sweetheart rode along with him; her attire was not at all costly.

CHAPTER 4

Erex now rode to that field on which the contest had been set up; he saw the pole and also the sparrow hawk, about which he had been told, and close by it his enemy on a fine stallion, as well as the knight's lady and the loathsome dwarf with the ugly face. A large crowd had by now also assembled there, yet no one dared attempt to claim the hawk for himself.

Erex then rode forward, grasped the pole, and called out in a loud voice, so that all who were present heard him: "I intend to carry off this pole, which I am holding onto, as well as the sparrow hawk which is attached to it, and I intend to defend it with my sword for the sake of my lady should anyone else dare to claim it."

At these words Malpirant rushed forward, greatly enraged. "Upon my word," he said, "you talk like a fool, for you shall pay dearly for this hawk. Both our lives as well as our possessions shall be at stake."

"But of course," said Erex, "come forward, if you dare. I certainly will not budge."

They now charged so hard at each other that all their saddle harness broke to pieces, and each knocked the other off his horse, although each landed on his feet. They then drew their swords and struck at each other fiercely; they struck such hard and strong blows that their shields shattered, their helmets cracked open, and their coats of mail were rent; each one of them was so wounded and tired that he could scarcely stand.

At this point Malpirant said to Erex: "Shall we rest?"

"No," replied Erex, "not before you receive from me many another strong blow and so lose your life, or else I myself lie dead here."

Then Erex raised his sword with both hands and split the knight's helmet and also a large part of the skull. At this blow Malpirant fell to the ground, while Erex pounced on him, ready to slay him.

"Have mercy on me, good knight," Malpirant said, "now that my life and possessions are in your power. My lady and I will serve you as long as we both live."

Erex replied: "Surely you are deserving of death because of that disgrace which your dwarf, whose brazenness went unpunished by you, brought upon me yesterday, and upon the lady with me. I am indeed that knight whom you saw in the clearing."

"I admit that I have done wrong," Malpirant answered; "nevertheless, I ask that you spare my life."

Erex said: "Since you have now come into my power and have surrendered, you must go at once to Castle Kardigan with your sweetheart and your dwarf, and hand yourself over to the queen, to receive such mercy as she may see fit to grant

you. Tell her that I shall arrive there tomorrow with my
sweetheart."

Malpirant agreed to this gladly and did not delay his
journey, since he wanted to keep his promise of good faith
and the pledge he had given Erex in regard to this. He left
the castle while his friends and kinsmen remained behind
grieving and bemoaning his defeat.

Malpirant rode now until he came to Castle Kardigan, to
the hall of the king, and dismounted. Gawain and Kay, the
steward of King Arthur, and many other knights were there;
they asked what had occurred, since they saw that his shield
had been shattered, his coat of mail rent, and he himself was
seriously wounded.

"Good fellows," he replied, "where is the queen, for I have
pressing business with her, matters to relate which will please
her. On my honor, I am bound to tell the news first to her."

Gawain now took him by the hand, and led him, together
with his sweetheart and dwarf, before the king and queen.
The knight greeted the king courteously, and then went
before the queen; he fell to his knee before her, greeted her
courteously and nobly, and then spoke up so that all heard
who were present.

"My lady, the queen," he said, "I have been vanquished and
overcome, and have been sent here with my sweetheart and
dwarf to receive such mercy as you might want to bestow. It is
Erex, that most valiant knight, who has overcome me in single
combat. He is now in good spirits in that castle which is called
Roson, and with him is his sweetheart whom he has just
recently married. She is so beautiful and well-bred that in the
whole wide world there is no other like her. Never before
have I been vanquished in single combat. Give quick judg-
ment now on our case—but more in keeping with your mercy
than our merit. I can furthermore tell you that Erex will come
here tomorrow with his beautiful sweetheart."

The queen spoke: "You are truly deserving of death be-
cause of that disgrace which your dwarf inflicted on my lady
in waiting and on my knight, and you are not deserving of
any mercy as far as we are concerned. But conquering one's
own anger and helping miserable wretches in need is the

greatest victory; therefore, stand up, knight, you and your party—you shall be welcome here."

He now thanked the queen for his life and for his freedom. The queen then ordered men to see to their horses and clothes, and they did so. She also had physicians come to heal his wounds, and this was done in all humility and with meek service. King Arthur later made him his retainer, and he was esteemed there and enjoyed great favor.

CHAPTER 5

Now the story returns to Erex, who was staying in the aforementioned castle after the duel with Malpirant. The earl who was lord of this castle was named Balsant and he invited Erex and many others to a feast and offered to give him whatever he wanted. Erex, however, wished to go back to the same lodgings as before—to his host and his sweetheart. When the earl perceived this, he and his men accompanied Erex, and the earl arranged a feast there at his own expense. All acclaimed Erex for his valiant deed.

Early the next day Erex got ready for his return journey. The earl provided him with a following of thirty knights and gave him two steeds as well as many other precious gifts, and accompanied Erex part of the way. They then parted as friends.

Erex and his lady now rode to the castle where King Arthur was holding court. The king himself went to meet them and lifted the maiden out of the saddle. The queen in turn took her under her care and in her generosity—which was by no means lacking—realized that the girl had need of her attention. The queen dressed her immediately in a tunic of costly material, which was magnificently adorned, and worth not less than ten marks of gold. In addition, the maiden received a cloak of precious material lined in white fur, striped with black sable, and trimmed with gold lace. The adornments cast off much radiance, yet an even greater brilliance came from the girl's hair than from all the gold lace.

The queen then took her by the hand and, accompanied by

her maidens, led her into the royal hall, into the presence of
the king, his court, and Erex. The king himself stood up to
meet the queen and the maiden, and he had the girl sit next
to him. He and all the retainers gazed at her and marveled at
her beauty. She had blushed somewhat, when she was led into
the hall, because she was ordinarily not used to being sur-
rounded by so many people. The color of her face was a
combination of the redness of a rose and the whiteness of a
lily, or of red blood in freshly fallen snow, or of the sun's
radiance in a cloudless sky. As she sat and as she walked her
movements, in fact all her behavior was most fitting.

The queen now addressed the king: "Any knight who has
performed such feats of bravery and valor, and has brought
such a maiden to our court, is worthy of great honor. There-
fore, let Erex be welcome here among us all."

"That is true," said the king, "and I have never seen a more
beautiful maiden. If it is acceptable to the retainers, and it is
the judgment of all that she can indeed be proclaimed the
most beautiful and most well-bred of all the maidens at our
court, then I will claim from her that kiss which I have earned
with my spear. Now give your fair decision on this matter and
award me the kiss."

Thus the king concluded his speech, and all cried out with
one voice and gave their judgment that because of her beauty
she alone was worthy to receive this boon.

Thereupon the king turned to the young girl and said:
"Lovely maiden, I give you this kiss not because of any guile
or evil intentions on my part, but rather in a spirit of sacred
love and with a pure heart. The kiss is your due, and is to be
above suspicion throughout our lives."

CHAPTER 6

Now after a short time had passed Erex asked King
Arthur for permission to hold his wedding. The king con-
sented gladly and at once sent a summons throughout all his
realm to kings and earls and other chieftains to assemble in
Lincoln during those days which some call Pentecost or Whit-

suntide. Refusal to appear would incur his wrath. Erex in turn sent thirty knights, supplied with good horses and precious garments, to fetch the father and mother of his sweetheart. He also sent word to his own father, King Ilax, requesting him to come to the wedding at the appointed time.

In answer to the king's summons there now assembled a great crowd of people, among them outstanding chieftains, whom I shall now enumerate. First there came King Ilax, the father of Erex, with four hundred smartly attired knights. Then there arrived King Variens of Sasiaborg with six hundred very well-dressed knights. Then came King Areta with his two sons, both excellent men, with a thousand brave knights. King Balldvin from Germaina came next with seven hundred knights, all of whom had long beards. None of them was under seventy years of age and they all carried either a grey or white hawk, a moulted falcon.

Then there arrived Sartinus, king of Rimul. He was young and handsome and accompanied by eight hundred knights, young men, none of whom had a beard. Then there came Erbilis, the king of the dwarfs, and himself a dwarf. He brought along five hundred dwarfs as well as his brothers Brattur and Revellus. They were followed by Earl Osester with two hundred knights; they came from Floresborg. Andigami arrived with four hundred knights, Gorgonus from Strialsborg with three hundred knights, and Earls Otun and Beralld with two hundred knights. These also were from Floresborg. Then there arrived Earl Masade with three hundred knights from that island which is called Vera, an island on which there is neither snake nor toad, and where it never gets too hot nor too cold, and where there is no winter. Garse and Jentaneon, mighty chieftains, arrived with their brother Earl Gorgun and with nine hundred knights. They were earls from Flandrisborg, which is in Flaemingialand. Thereupon came fifty dukes, among them Langalif, Stanes, and his brother Stenes; Gasadin, Casain, and Cleines; Roddan and Rivalld, and the mighty Ascamint, as well as many other chieftains. They were accompanied by three thousand knights.[1]

Now there had gathered at King Arthur's court a great crowd of people who had come together from far and wide throughout the world. And when the king looked over this assemblage, the thought came to him that his power and might were great, since such a great part of the world, including mighty chieftains and excellent lords, was subject to him, and he rejoiced in his heart. Yet he did not pride himself on his power to which so many vassals were subject. He now brought gladness and honor to all those who had come to him, and arranged the wedding with great pomp and festivities. He dubbed many a young man knight and gave special weapons, excellent suits of clothes, and good horses to them all. There was no lack of gaiety and good cheer.

Now when the wedding day arrived, the maiden was asked for her name, as is prescribed by God's law, and it turned out that her name was Evida; Erex had not known her name before this. The archbishop of Canterbury joined them in matrimony, and the wedding day passed with rejoicing. In the evening, the queen led the maiden to bed, while kings and earls and bishops and other noble chieftains led Erex. Then their marriage was consecrated with prayers and all kinds of ceremony.

The wedding festivities, which were most pleasant and enjoyable lasted for over half a month. And when the festivities came to an end, the chieftains were dismissed with precious gifts; not a single person left without some. Before the chieftains left, however, Gawain asked King Arthur to delay the departures for a week so that they could hold a tournament for the enjoyment of all those who had gathered there. The knights would have an opportunity to test their prowess and chivalric ability, and those who achieved the greatest renown might earn the king's praise. King Arthur agreed to this and invited everyone to be his guests. Many a knight there was outfitted with good horses and with gold-worked garments and with excellent weapons ornamented in gold.

The most intense jousting began, and in all that host not one was found to equal Erex except Sir Gawain; they were equals in knighthood. And now they earned fame and praise from the king and queen and from all the chieftains, and, moreover, from all the common people. This tournament ended in such a way that the chieftains parted in friendship, and each went home to his own realm.

CHAPTER 7

Erex then asked the king and queen to give him leave to go home to his father's kingdom, since he had been gone for a long time. The king and queen granted this request, providing him with a suitable escort, and he parted from them with great honor and in friendship. Erex then rode with his wife to his father's castle, and King Ilax himself, accompanied by learned men and his retainers left the castle to meet his son in procession and to lead him, amidst joyful celebration, into the castle hall. An excellent banquet had been prepared there.

Now after these events Erex settled down to a life of ease. He was so in love with his sweetheart that he gave up all the conviviality and diversion found in the company of young men. Although he was esteemed by all his countrymen, he nevertheless brought upon himself some reproach for his complacent way of life.

It distressed his wife to hear others speak harshly of him and one morning, as she was lying in bed beside her husband and thought that he was sleeping, she spoke in a low voice to herself, and said: "It grieves me, my lord, that you are being reproached because of your love for me and the easy life you are leading."

Erex heard her words and immediately jumped up, dressed, and said to her: "Get dressed at once in your best clothes, for this day both of us will ride forth from this castle. No longer do I intend to endure reproach from my countrymen for my life of ease."

Evida now regretted having spoken, but she dressed hastily and with great sadness. In the meantime Erex took his armor and their horses, saddled them, and then lifted his wife onto her horse. Then he went to his father and told him of his plans. Although the king and all the retainers were greatly grieved at his course of action, they nevertheless were unable to keep him from carrying out his plans. So Erex jumped on his horse and rode away from there with no other company but his wife. Since he had threatened with death anyone who wanted to follow him, no one dared to do so.

He rode now towards Herford woods, through which roamed eight robbers who plundered and killed men. Thus they ravaged the highways and inflicted great harm on many a one. Erex bade his lady ride before him and to pay no attention to any danger they might encounter; moreover, she was not to speak to him. They rode for a long time through the forest before they saw a castle. In front of it were three knights, armed and on good horses; they were amusing themselves. Erex realized that they were robbers.

Now when the people who were in the castle saw Erex and Evida approaching, they called to their companions to inform them that they could see a well-equipped knight accompanied by a fair maiden. One of them then spoke: "Upon my word, since I'm your leader I have first choice from our booty, and thus I claim his lady."

The second man spoke up: "I shall get his sword," and the third: "His coat of mail shall fall to me."

"His shield and spear will be mine," said the fourth, and the fifth: "I shall get his helmet, banner, and purse."

The sixth in turn spoke: "I shall get all his clothes," and the seventh said: "His horse and saddle harness fall to me."

But the eighth spoke up: "You're wronging me by not sharing the loot fairly with me. Since I am not getting any property, I claim his right hand and foot, in fact his life."

Now the three who were already dressed for combat advanced toward Erex, while those who were in the castle armed themselves in order to be ready to come to the aid of their companions, if need be.

Evida now saw how these three were riding towards them and that they were acting in a threatening manner. She remembered that Erex had bidden her to keep silence, but she could not do so because of her love for him. She was far ahead of him and so she now turned back to tell him what she saw. For that she was reproached by him.

As soon as they met up with Erex, one of the robbers thrust at his shield, yet did not cut into it deeply; rather the lance rebounded and sank into the ground. When the robber bent down after it, Erex struck him so forcefully on the neck with his lance that his opponent's eyes flew out of his head. With that he fell to the ground unconscious and Erex's horse trampled him underfoot until he was dead. Then the second robber struck so hard at Erex's shield that the sword stuck fast; Erex twisted his shield in such a way that the other lost his sword. Then Erex struck him so hard on the head with the rim of his shield that the robber's brains spilled out. As the third one retreated, Erex hurled his lance at him and pierced him through, and he fell dead to the ground. At this moment their five companions approached and the fiercest battle ensued. Erex slew them all, but he himself was little wounded. Erex then took their weapons, clothes, and horses and rode with his wife into the castle, which was now totally uninhabited, and they slept there that night.

CHAPTER 8

Early the next morning, after having securely locked the castle, Erex and Evida rode away from there with eight horses. They were loaded down with booty, yet even more was left behind. His lady rode ahead and Erex followed, driving the horses. They traveled in this manner for many days, sleeping at night in the open, until they came to a castle, Pulchra by name, which was ruled by Earl Milon. That night Erex and Evida lodged with a yeoman in the castle.

Everyone there who saw her marveled at Evida's beauty. Report of this reached the earl, who went at once to meet Evida and Erex. Although he did not know them, he received them with pleasure, and they sat down side by side. The earl could not take his eyes off Evida.

He thought his heart would burn up for love of her, and he spoke to her in secret: "Listen to me, fairest woman in all the world, your beauty overpowers all the might of this earth—praised be God for knowing how to create such a beautiful being—and because of your beauty my heart is being consumed by fire. You must become my lady and rule my realm as you please."

"May God keep you," she said, "you are a powerful chieftain, appointed by God to exalt his Christianity and to punish the unrighteous, but I am bound in holy matrimony. You would not wish to rob the Creator of two souls at the same time and thus to damn yourself and me for eternity."

"I am so overcome by this desire," replied the earl, "that I would not give up your love for all the gold in the world, and I intend to marry you and to cut off your husband's head, even though God's wrath come upon me for that. Don't tell me you are so mad and senseless that you think it better to follow an impoverished impostor and vagabond than to sit on a throne beside me, and to rule over my whole realm with me."

Evida was now greatly distressed, but she quickly hit upon a good plan. She said to him: "Sir, I believe you when you say that you desire me, and therefore I will gladly do whatever you want, provided you will abide by my plan. Let Erex and me sleep together in peace tonight, so that I don't appear to be consenting to his slaying. In the morning have me taken away from him—I will thus have a better case for my innocence—and then do with him what you please. But promise to keep your word to me and give me your signet ring as a token of your pledge."

The earl gladly agreed to this and gave her his ring. Then he departed with his men.

That night, as soon as Erex and Evida were in bed, she told him of her conversation with the earl and showed him the signet ring as proof. They immediately dressed and got ready to leave. They gave the yeoman a good charger for his hospitality and then rode out of the place. When the earl found out about this, he and his counselor Bolvin quickly armed themselves, as did also his knights, a hundred in all, and they rode in hot pursuit of Erex. On a plain near a forest they came upon him. By this time the earl and his counselor were far ahead of their troops.

Evida now called Erex's attention to the pursuit, but he reproached her for this. Nonetheless, he turned back to thrust his spear through Bolvin, and flung him dead from his horse. At that Earl Milon approached and thrust at Erex with all his might, striking so hard at his shield that it split in two. Erex surely would have been slain, had his coat of mail not protected him; nevertheless, he was severely wounded. Erex now cut off the earl's spearshaft and then struck his helmet such a blow that he not only cut off all the copper from the helmet, but also the earl's hair, some of his skin, and an ear as well. The sword landed on the shoulder and cut off everything in its path, so that the earl also lost an arm. At this the earl fell unconscious off the horse and onto the ground, while Erex escaped into the forest.

The earl's men now reached the spot where he was lying; some crowded around him while others rode in pursuit of Erex. At this point the earl regained consciousness and called out in a loud voice, asking his men not to be so bold as to ride after Erex and do him harm.

Then he spoke as follows: "God has shown his justice to me in this matter, for I not only wanted to kill Erex, but also to disgrace and thus harm his wife. Instead it has turned out for me that my best friend and highest counselor is dead and I myself am wounded. May God's will be done; it is up to Him whether I go on living or not. In any case, I will not seek vengeance and they shall go in peace, as far as I'm concerned." Having said this, the earl turned to go home.

That day Erex rode on his way through the forest and when evening came he and Evida settled down for the night in a clearing. There Erex bound up his wounds. The next morning they rode out of the forest and past a castle. Out of this castle rode a knight so large and strong that Erex thought he had never seen anyone like him. He rode a fine steed and all his weapons were ornamented with gold. The horse's trappings were of a precious material and his standard of baldachin, which was shot all over with gold. He rode hard at Erex and addressed him: "You, knight, give me your beautiful sweetheart, because it is most fitting that she should be mine. I desire to have her and am willing to stake my life on it."

"I am seriously wounded," Erex replied, "and thus little capable of hand-to-hand combat, but I would sooner fight than give up my sweetheart, because I am more in the right."

Hereupon the fiercest struggle ensued and they jousted so hard that they both slid backwards off their horses but landed on their feet on the ground. They quickly drew their swords and struck vehemently at each other until they were so exhausted and wounded that they could scarcely raise their swords. At last they went down onto their knees, and thus it continued. Evida wept sorely now, when she saw the fate of her husband; at times she even fell into a faint because of her grief.

The man from the castle now suggested that they take a rest and asked Erex for his name, but Erex said that his opponent ought to tell first who he was, and the stranger obliged.

"I am a king," he said, "so rich in lands and possessions that four earls, seven counts, and many other great men are my vassals. My name is Guimar and I am the son of the sister of King Ilax. But now tell me your name, for I have never met a better knight than you."

Erex now told him his name as well as that of his father and family. Then Guimar cast down his sword, threw his arms around the neck of Erex, and welcomed him as a friend. He begged him not to be angry at him and offered to share all his goods with him. Because of their kinship Erex forgot all his anger and he and Evida rode home with Guimar to the castle. They stayed there for a half a month. Erex's wounds healed now, and as soon as he had recovered, he got ready to depart. He did not wish to have an escort, but Erex asked his kinsman to grant him assistance if he should ever need it, and Guimar gladly agreed. They parted in friendship, but it grieved King Guimar that Erex did not wish to take along any of his men, since he would still have many an obstacle to surmount.

CHAPTER 9

Erex and Evida now rode for many days until they came to a desolate forest. It was large and dense, but they found shelter for the night in a clearing. At midnight they heard loud weeping and hideous sounds. Erex got up, took his armor and his horse, and followed these sounds until he came upon a woman running about the forest weeping, tearing off her clothes, and pulling at her hair.

He asked her why she was weeping and she replied: "I used to be a wealthy woman and was married to an excellent husband. He and I were in high spirits as we rode into this forest accompanied by twenty knights. But then yesterday evening two giants came upon us. They killed all the knights, but my husband they seized forcibly; they beat him, and bound his hands behind him. I managed to get away. Now I am a poor, miserable wretch, for the giants also took our horses and other possessions. Now they can only be a short distance from here. It is impossible to deal with these giants, and although you cannot do any better, at least pity me my grief."

"Don't cry, dear woman," Erex replied, "and wait for me here. I will indeed ride after them and try to see what I can accomplish."

He then lifted Evida off her horse; she was sorrowful upon hearing her husband's plan, but she could not dissuade him. Erex now charged as fast as possible into the forest and soon he could see two giants. One of them was driving many horses loaded with good weapons and other precious treasures, while the other rode much farther behind with a horse on a lead. On this horse was a stark naked man with his hands tied behind his back and his feet tied together under the horse's belly. He was close to death for he had been so beaten and badly flogged that both horse and man were dripping with blood.

Erex turned to the giant who was with the man and addressed him: "Good sir, if you will free that man who is in such a sorry state, you will be rewarded with my friendship."

In reply the giant looked grimly at him and said: "Get lost, you loathsome scoundrel, if you wish to stay alive, for you will never be able to rescue this man from me."

"I am certainly going to rescue him, if I can," Erex responded.

The giant laughed in his face and said: "You're a fool and talk like an idle braggart. You are no more a match for me than is a lamb for a lion."

At this Erex struck at the giant's shoulder with his sword. It cut right through his chest and came out on the other side and Erex cast him dead from his horse. At this moment his companion came up, swung high a large iron club, and struck at Erex. With his shield Erex warded off the blow with all his might, but was nevertheless severely injured. The blow struck the horse on the neck and it fell dead to the ground. Although he was not directly hit, Erex still was stunned and tumbled to the ground. When the giant saw this, he raised up his club with all his strength intending to strike Erex on the head and cause his brains to spill out. But Erex jumped to his feet and dodged between the giant's feet. The force of the blow was such that the club sank right into the ground as far up as his hands, so that the giant was completely bent over. Now Erex raised his sword with all his might and struck the giant on the back, cutting him in half.

After this he untied the bound knight. Erex asked him his name, and the knight fell to the ground at his feet, thanked him handsomely for freeing him and saving his life, and then said: "My name is Kalviel; I am by birth from Karinlisborg and am duke of Folkborg. My sweetheart's name is Favida, the daughter of Earl Ubbi of Buderisborg. My sweetheart and I will serve you for life and do whatever you bid us."

Erex thanked him for his offer, but said that he did not wish to enslave someone whom God himself had rescued in his mercy. Instead he asked the knight to ride to King Arthur and to tell him the truth about his exploits. The knight gladly agreed to do so. Then they took their horses and all the booty which the giants had been traveling around with and rode off to find their sweethearts. After a very joyous reunion the two couples parted in friendship.

Kalviel rode to the court of King Arthur where he told the king of Erex's exploits. The king and his retainers were cheered at this report and rejoiced over Erex's extraordinary bravery.

CHAPTER 10

The story now returns to Erex and his sweetheart; they had been riding about in the forest for a long time. Fruit from the trees was their only nourishment. One day they heard terrible noises and immediately thereafter they saw a winged dragon flying along with a fully armed man dangling from its jaws. Although the dragon had swallowed him to beyond the waist, the man was still alive, and the dragon flew rather low because the man was heavy. Erex was distressed now at the thought that such a splendid fellow should die in such a manner and he appealed to God with all his heart for help in saving the life of that man.

Then he rode toward the dragon with fearless heart, for he preferred to lose his own life rather than not to try to help that man. Erex struck at the dragon—which recoiled from the blow—and cut off its shoulder. At this the dragon let go of the man and turned upon Erex, hurling itself at him with gaping jaws. But Erex leaped off his horse and with all his might he thrust his lance into the mouth of the dragon, all the way down to its heart. The dragon then fell dead on top of Erex's horse, causing it to die on the spot. Erex and his lady Evida now went over to the man who lay unconscious on the ground, rather close to death, and they tried to revive him as best they could. When he regained consciousness he thanked Erex heartily for saving his life.

When they asked him for his name he replied: "My name is Plato. I am duke of Margdeiborg, and the son of the sister of Sir Gawain, who is a member of King Arthur's court. This dragon seized me while I was sleeping this morning on my shield. It happened a short distance away from here and my lady and servants are searching for me there. I give myself and all my kingdom into your power."

Erex now thanked Almighty God for having rescued through him such an excellent knight. The two now fully realized that they knew each other, and a most joyful recognition scene took place there.

Plato's sweetheart in the meantime was very sad at his disappearance and thought that he was dead. When she and Plato's men arrived on the spot, they saw that he was free and alive. No words can tell how happy they became when they found out what had happened, and falling at the feet of Erex they thanked him eloquently for this victory and his act of charity. Moreover, they offered to accompany and serve him, which he immediately refused. He asked them instead to go to King Arthur and to tell the king what had happened on their journey. Although they were unwilling to leave him, they agreed to do so. Thus they parted from him for the time being.

Erex and his sweetheart continued riding through the forest and had done so for a long time when they saw seven men, mounted and fully armed. They were driving many horses toward a certain castle which stood a short distance away. Some of the horses were loaded with precious treasures but others carried four knights, who were bound and wounded, and four very lovely young ladies. When the men driving the horses saw Erex riding along, three immediately turned toward him while the other four rode on to the castle to take care of their booty.

The leader of the group called out to Erex in a loud voice: "You, knight! You're a fool for riding right into our hands. If you wish to stay alive, hand over to us your weapons, clothing, and sweetheart. Then you can leave barefoot in your underwear and be eternally grateful to us for sparing your life."

"These alternatives are not equal choices," Erex responded; "you'll have to buy my life dearly before I agree to such."

At this Erex rode at them and thrust his lance through the chest of one of them, casting him dead from his horse. With his sword in his right hand he struck at the second one, slashing his face and cutting into the helmet so that his skull split and his brains spilled down onto the ground. The third one fled when he saw his companions fall, but he too quickly received death, for Erex struck him on the back in such a manner that he was cut in two in the middle. The other four now came at him, all riding at Erex at the same time. Their leader alone was worse to deal with than the other three together. Now Erex not only received many grievous wounds but the old ones opened up again. But Erex slew them all, and thus the fight came to an end, but not before he was greatly overcome by his wounds and exhaustion. Nevertheless he rode quickly to the castle where the men were bound and untied them. Then he asked them for their names.

The one who was at their head said: "I am Juben, duke of Forckheim, and these three are my brothers—Perant, Joachim, and Malcheus, the dukes of Manaheim. The ladies are our sweethearts. We had heard about these criminals and intended to free these roads of them and thus to put our fame to the test. Since you have saved our lives and freed us, we—as well as our knights—now very much wish to serve you."

"Good sirs," Erex replied, "may God's peace be with you because of your offer, but I do not desire your service. But if you wish to do something to further my honor, then go quickly to King Arthur and tell him that Erex, the son of Ilax, has rescued you."

Their leader agreed gladly to this and asked Erex to dismount, bind up his wounds, and rest there with them for a while. But Erex did not wish to do that. Instead he turned to go back into the forest with Evida. They wanted to follow him but he forbade them to do so. So they returned to the castle, where they bound up their wounds; they stayed several nights before riding off to meet King Arthur.

CHAPTER 11

The story now relates that Erex and his lady rode out of the forest and came to a green meadow. By now he was losing so much blood from his wounds that he became unconscious and fell from his horse. His unconsciousness lasted so long, that Evida thought him dead and began to bewail her lot. She cried grievously, lay down covering his body with her own, and gave expression to her grief.

"How wretched I am now that my husband is dead. It is my tongue which brought him on this journey, my tongue, which was not silent at the unjust reproach of evil men. How can I ever go on living, grieving as I do for such a husband? Since I cannot do so, I shall find a quick death on his sword."

In her sorrow she wept so loudly that it could be heard at a great distance. She started to draw the sword and wanted to raise it by the hilt, but the sword was so heavy that she could scarcely lift it off the ground. She kept hurting her fingers on the sword so that she had to let go time and again. Finally she thought of letting herself fall right onto the sword.

At this very moment a certain powerful earl, Placidus by name, approached on horseback, accompanied by a large following. He and his men realized what danger her life was in and removed the sword. They did not think it wise for her to lose both life and soul and thereby forfeit the kingdom of heaven. The earl tried to comfort her by saying that with her beauty and noble bearing she would quickly find an even better husband, but Evida only scorned his words. The earl now ordered his men to make ready a bier right there in the forest. As soon as this was accomplished, the body was carried home to the earl's hall, and there it was honorably displayed.

The earl now had Evida sit on the throne beside him and was eager to talk with her. He did not even know her name, yet he offered himself to her in marriage and his kingdom besides to rule as she wished. Evida flatly refused his proposition. The earl wanted to bed her so badly that he felt as though ignited by sparks of fire. He asked the chaplain to marry them on the spot, but his retainers told him that it would be contrary to God's law unless Evida herself gave permission to do so—and *that* they could not get out of her.

The earl now resorted to demonstrating his great love for her. On the spot he had everyone invited to a feast. Tables were set up and the hall was filled with the earl's retainers as well as with townsmen. The earl had gold, jewels, and all kinds of treasures placed before Evida. Thus he coaxed her in every way he could. Evida rejected everything, however, and refused his attentions, declaring that he would never become her husband. At this the earl became angry. He boxed her ears and ordered her to eat with her new husband. Evida was weeping sorely by now, and a great tumult arose in the hall because the retainers were displeased by the earl's behavior.

At this moment Erex started to regain consciousness. When he saw Evida and realized what was going on, he did not like it at all; he leaped from the bier and drew his sword. He struck the earl on the head so that his brains spattered on the floor of the hall. When they saw what was happening, great fear came over the retainers. They rushed out of the hall as fast as they could.

"Let's get out of here as quickly as we can," they cried. "A devil is in that corpse for it has killed the earl." They ran away and hid as best they could.

Erex and his lady hurried out of the hall, quickly found their horses in the courtyard, mounted, and left the castle. They rode rapidly all that day and into the night until they stopped for shelter in a beautiful meadow, near a spring. Evida now bandaged Erex's wounds, and then they went to sleep. When day came, they took their horses and rode to a certain castle where they stayed for three days and rested.

Leaving the castle they rode a long way. One day a knight came riding along, whom Erex recognized as Kay, King Arthur's steward. Kay did not recognize Erex, however, and as soon as they met, Kay challenged him to joust with him. Although Erex was greatly wounded, he did not wish to refuse the challenge. In the first charge Erex unhorsed Kay, the steward, and took his horse intending to keep it for himself. Now Kay recognized Erex by his armor. He asked him to return the horse, but Erex refused to do so until Kay had told him that the horse really belonged to Gawain. Then they parted for the time being.

CHAPTER 12

Now the story relates that Erex and his lady proceeded on their way and found a place for the night in a clearing. Here Erex lost his strength completely.

Turning to Evida he said: "For quite some time now we have engaged in many a struggle, but God has sustained us throughout. Moreover, I have experienced your true love, virtue, and faithfulness. But now I suspect that death will soon part us, for I suffer greatly from my grievous wounds and from continuous lack of food."

So saying Erex fell into unconsciousness. Seeing this Evida wept sorely. At this very moment King Guimar, accompanied by many knights, approached on horseback, and immediately recognized Erex and Evida. Consoling Evida, he had Erex laid in a comfortable vehicle to convey him home to his castle, which was only a short distance away. There Guimar and his sister Godilna, who could cure anything, looked after Erex's wounds and he recovered quickly. Erex enjoyed Guimar's hospitality, but when his wounds were fully healed he asked the king for leave to depart. Guimar granted him this but wished to accompany him. This offer Erex accepted.

As escort King Guimar gave Erex thirty fully armed knights and presented him with a fine steed. This horse had come from Lombardy where it had been bought for twenty marks of gold. To Evida King Guimar gave a handsome palfrey carrying a golden saddle extensively set with magnificent jewels. The bridle, the saddle girth, and the stirrups were also made of gold. So skillful was the man who had made all this that on the saddlebow he had engraved all the wondrous deeds of the men of Troy.

The saddlecloth was of a costly white material filigreed with gold. Everything had been fashioned with such skill that the fastest, the best, the leading craftsman in all of Brittany could not have completed it in less than seven years. In addition to the horse Evida received an excellent set of clothes worth not less than sixty marks of gold.

They all rode out together amidst great merriment. After a journey of many days they arrived at a fortified town, sturdily built and surrounded by strong walls. This stronghold was called Bardiga and was ruled by King Effuen. Now King Guimar did not wish to approach it and Erex inquired as to the reason for this.

"There is a certain place in this fortress," Guimar responded, "which is called 'Joy of the Court,' but many a knight has found no joy there, many a one who has inquired about the nature of the inhabitants of that place. Not a single person who has gone there in the last seven years—however brave a knight he might be—has returned from there. This place about which you inquire is within the fortress and it too is surrounded by strong walls. If we ride into the stronghold I fear that you will want to go there."

"Of course I have to go there," replied Erex, "for this name has such a reputation. Besides, one only knows oneself by testing oneself."

CHAPTER 13

Now they rode into the fortified town and pro-
ceeded to the king's court where they were well received. King
Effuen himself went out to meet them and led them to his
hall. There he gave an excellent feast for them.

Erex now wanted to know where the place called "Joy of
the Court" might be. He told the king that his purpose was to
test himself in that place, in order to see whether he might
not thereby be able to advance his fame. He asked leave to go
there and added that he would consider it a disgrace if he
were denied permission to do so.

"I don't wish to conceal from you," the king responded,
"that many a man has been killed because of this very request.
In the last seven years everyone who has asked to go there has
lost his life. I am willing to give you half my kingdom to
insure that you never go there. If, however, neither my gifts
nor words can keep you from setting out on this journey, then
do as you please."

Erex thanked the king for the offer he made, but said that
he nevertheless wished to find out who lived in that place.
The king became sad at this but even more so Evida. In fact,
the general good cheer ceased. Everyone then retired for the
night.

In the morning Erex armed himself and then leaped on his
horse. The king and all his retainers accompanied him to the
place Erex had inquired about, where they parted from him
sorrowfully and with great concern. They asked God to have
mercy on him.

A high stone wall surrounded the place called "Joy of the
Court," and there was a gate with a strong iron door, which
was locked. But when anyone wished to enter, it was immedi-
ately opened by the gatekeeper, a dwarf. All along the wall
were many poles and on top of these were men's heads
anointed with a special salve to prevent decay. Many a person
could find some dear friend here.

Erex rode on through the gate accompanied by his lady.
Inside the wall was a beautiful field littered with many a

broken shield, coat of mail, and cloven helmet. Erex and Evida kept on riding until they came to a very beautiful garden in which stood a tent woven out of gold and samite. In this tent stood a bed of pure silver skillfully ornamented. A woman sat on this bed. She was so beautiful that it seemed to Erex that he had never seen anyone more beautiful except Evida. Erex and Evida stopped when they saw this scene. At this moment a tall, strong knight in full armor came riding at them.

He addressed Erex in abusive language: "Who are you, so foolhardy and impudent," he said, "as to intend to steal from me my property and my sweetheart? An evil intention has led many a man to seek death here, and that will also be your fate."

To this Erex replied: "What good are boastful words? Real men fight with weapons, not insults. But if you are eager to be rough, then you will get the same in return."

Some very hard jousting now began. Each broke his lance on his opponent, yet neither of them was knocked out of the saddle by the other. They then leaped from their horses to fight with their swords and each now struck strong blows at the other. They became so tired and wounded that they could scarcely stand on their feet. The battle ended when the knight who had challenged Erex fell and asked for quarter. Erex granted this and then asked his opponent for his name.

"Mabanaring is my name," he said, "and I spent a long time at the court of the famous King Ilax. At her own wish I took the young lady you see sitting here away from her father, Earl Tracon of Acusborg, a great and powerful champion. I had pledged to grant her whatever she requested, and I did so when she asked me to take her to this place. I was to stay here and not part from her until I was vanquished by another knight. She thought that would never happen. Her reason for asking this was that she thought she would be disgraced if people found out that her lover was only a knight. Moreover, she feared that her father would overpower me with his host if he found out my whereabouts. Be so good now as to tell me your name so that I may know who has vanquished me."

Erex now recognized Mabanaring and told him his own

name as well as that of his father. A very joyful scene took place, for Evida recognized in the lady her own kinswoman Elena; the two were daughters of brothers. Later they all left this place and rode to the king's court, where their arrival— that of the king and all those with him—was greeted with much joy. Everyone now praised Erex for his valor and chivalrous deeds.

CHAPTER 14

When the time came to depart Erex thanked King Effuen for his great hospitality and the king led Erex and Evida with proper honor out of his court. After a journey of ten days Erex and Evida arrived at Castle Kardigan. Both King Arthur and the queen were present. Amidst great joy the king himself, accompanied by all his retainers, went to meet the couple. Welcoming Erex as well as King Guimar and all their company, King Arthur led them to his hall. He had Erex sit next to him on the throne while Evida and her kinswoman Elena were given places next to the queen.

King Arthur then asked Erex for information concerning his various journeys, even though he already knew about many of Erex's valiant deeds. Erex told about everything that had happened to him in detail. The king was greatly impressed by his valor and the retainers joined in praising his illustrious bravery.

Mabanaring now stepped forward and approached King Arthur. Falling at the king's feet, Mabanaring told him the story of his life. The knight surrendered himself into the king's power and asked for mercy, and because Erex interceded for him, it was granted. Moreover, Mabanaring became a member of Arthur's court, where he proved to be the best knight in all perilous undertakings and quickly won great esteem because of his valor.

King Arthur then turned his attention to Erex. "Sir Erex," he said, "you have proven yourself in many dangerous situations, in all of which God has sustained you. I now advise you to give up your hard toils for a time in order to indulge in some rest and leisure. I must, however, inform you that King Ilax, your father, has died. Consequently his kingdom stands unguarded against many kinds of danger and hostility. Therefore, I want you, first of all, to take as many of my men as you will need and ride home with them to secure your kingdom. Then, at Christmas, come back to me and bring along from your realm the archbishop and the other chieftains. You will then be consecrated king."

Erex agreed to do what King Arthur had suggested and thanked him gratefully for his wise counsel and for the surpassing friendship which the king had shown him.

After a time Erex took leave of the king and queen to ride home to his kingdom. He brought peace to it and made it secure. Then he summoned all the chieftains of his land into his presence and together they set out for the court of King Arthur. In accordance with the king's invitation, Erex arrived with a large following on Christmas Eve. They were warmly welcomed by the king and queen. Then all were entertained at a sumptuous feast: kings and dukes, earls and barons, counts and knights—they were all present together with a host of many thousands of followers. Christmas Eve thus passed with great pomp and merriment.

On Christmas Day Erex was consecrated king by seven archbishops and thirteen suffragan bishops who assisted in the ceremony. Evida was consecrated in the same manner. In the course of the consecration Erex received from King Arthur a golden crown, set with magnificent jewels, which had been bought in Africa for no less than thirty marks of gold, and the king himself placed it on Erex's head. To Evida King Arthur gave a magnificent, glittering cloak on which were depicted the seven liberal arts. The cloak had been woven by four elfwomen nine leagues under the earth in an underground room which never saw daylight. So costly was this cloak that not even a merchant would be able to estimate its value.

When the ceremonies had been concluded, Erex and Evida were led back to the hall with honor. Then everyone proceeded to table: the chieftains—none of whom ranked below kings and archbishops, dukes and suffragan bishops, barons and counts—were assigned seats of honor in twelve halls; the host of knights and the other people were assigned to other quarters and to the gardens found within the castle walls. Nevertheless, it was still necessary to pitch tents outside for those people, many thousands of them, whom the castle could not hold. From all this one can get some idea how many people had come together there. In addition, there were three thousand servants. Every form of entertainment one can think of was available to gladden the people.

The feasting went on for a full month. At the end of that time King Arthur dismissed the chieftains, sending them away with splendid gifts. They all thanked Arthur as well as the queen for having provided such a splendid feast and then rode home to their kingdoms.

King Erex and Queen Evida then also parted from King Arthur and his queen expressing their friendship—it was to last as long as they lived. From there they rode home to their kingdom and ruled it with honor and glory during a period of complete peace.

They had two sons, one of whom was named Odus, after Evida's father, and the other Ilax, after Erex's father. Both of them became kings. They were distinguished men, valiant and chivalrous like their father. When Erex died they inherited the kingdom.

Here ends the saga of that excellent King Erex and his lady, the beautiful Evida.

ÍVENS
SAGA

Royal MS. 14 E. III, f. 89. King Arthur feasting at Pentecost, waiting for an adventure to be told. Reproduced by permission of the British Library Board.

This is the story of that excellent knight Íven who was one of King Arthur's champions.

The excellent King Arthur ruled over England—as many are aware—and finally became emperor of Rome. He was the most famous of all those kings who have ruled on this side of the ocean and the most popular after Charlemagne. He had the bravest knights in all Christendom.

One time he summoned, as was his custom, all his friends, those most excellent people, to hold a great feast at Pentecost, which we call Whitsuntide. While the king was sitting on his throne, and everyone was having a very good time, such a great drowsiness came over the king that he could do nothing else but go to his quarters for a nap. All the people were surprised by this because he had never done such a thing before. The queen was with him in his quarters. In front of the bedroom door were sitting the king's knights Lancelot, Kalebrant, Sigamor, Gawain, Íven, and Kay. When they got bored sitting there, they began drawing lots to see who should tell the story of one of his adventures. The lot fell to Kalebrant; so he began a certain story which was more to his disgrace than to his honor. The queen heard this and went out to ask him to tell the story so that she might hear it too.

Kalebrant replied: "I would rather suffer great distress than tell you anything about it. Yet I do not desire to anger you. I shall do as you request, if you will do as I say. Be perceptive and apply your ears, because words which we hear are lost at once if our minds do not attend to what our ears are receiving. There are all too many people who praise what they do not bother to understand. They don't get any more out of it than what they hear; their minds forget to comprehend. Like the wind which blows but does not stop anywhere, so too go those words which we hear—unless our minds are awake to receive those words. Let those who wish to understand my words apply both their ears and their hearts. I certainly do not intend to tell them a dream or a lie, or even that which there is some doubt about, but rather just what I experienced and saw."

CHAPTER 2

"Now it happened seven years ago, as I was riding all alone, deep in thought, armed in full armor as befits a knight, that I came upon a road leading into the forest, which was very dense and thick with brambles. I rode all day and at evening came out of the forest. I saw a little hazel grove and rode toward it. Then I saw a castle of wood with a deep moat around it. On the bridge to the castle stood a knight who owned the castle. He invited me to take lodgings there, and I accepted his offer. As I entered his hall, I saw a plate of bell metal there. My host then took a hammer which was hanging there and struck the plate three times so that the people who were up in the tower heard the sound and came down at once into the courtyard and took my horse.

"Then there came toward me a girl, very lovely in form, created according to all one's desires, and royally dressed. My heart beheld her eagerly. She at once took my armor from me and dressed me in rich apparel of good scarlet cloth trimmed with white fur. All the people left us then so that we were alone together. And indeed, I was eager to see no one but her. She led me to a lovely grassy field, so fair that I don't think another of equal beauty exists in the whole world. There was there the scent of the best balsam. I found her to be so courteous, so fine-mannered, so fitting, so pleasant of word, so cheerful and yet humble that I would never have left if I could have had my way.

"It seemed to me most distressing then, when the mighty lord of the castle came to look for me. The preparations for supper were completed, and I could remain no longer because it was mealtime. I did as the lord bade me. I need not say much about the supper since I could have wished for nothing better. The girl sat down before me and also ate. When the knight was full, he told me it had been a long time since he had lodged a knight such as me who was out in search of adventure, although he often received many people. He asked me to visit him again on my way back, and I answered that I would be glad to do that. The night was bright, and the sky clear.

"At dawn my horse was ready, as I had requested of my host. I thanked the knight and his beautiful daughter for the bounteous hospitality and took leave of them. I rode away and after a little while found in a thicket some wild bulls and leopards which were fighting and roaring terribly. I stopped and saw a hideous black man who was sitting on a tree stump. He held a large iron sledge hammer in his hand. His head was bigger than that of an ass. All his hair stood straight up. His forehead was bald and two spans broad. His ears were very big, with hair growing inside. He had coal-black eyes, a crooked nose, and a mouth as broad as a lion's. His teeth were large and sharp, like a wild boar's. He had a lot of hair and a beard like a horse's tail. His chin had grown together with his chest. He had a long hunched back and leaned forward on his sledge hammer. His clothing was neither of wool nor of linen, but instead he had two recently flayed bull's hides fastened about him.

"He jumped up onto a tree stump eight ells high, when he saw me, and stared at me but did not speak. For that reason I thought he was witless. However, I gathered my courage and asked: 'Are you a human being, or a spirit, or some other creature?'

"He answered: 'I am a human being such as you now see. I never change my shape.'²

"I then asked him what he was doing in the forest.

"'I'm taking care of these beasts which you see here,' he replied.

"I asked him how he could take care of them when they were so savage and far-roaming.

"He said: 'As soon as they see me, they don't dare move. If

any one of them wants to run away, I rush after it and seize it by the horns with my big, tough fists and tear its head off. As soon as I catch one of them, the others will shake with terror and dread, and then they all gather around me, as if they were begging me for mercy. However, if anyone else goes toward them they kill him at once. In that way I am the master of the beasts here. But what sort of a person are you?'

"I replied that I was a knight seeking adventures in which I might make trial of my valor and knighthood. 'I ask you to tell me what you know concerning such matters.'

"He answered that he had never heard the word *adventures* before. 'However, if you ride a short distance from here to a certain spring, then you will not leave there without danger, unless you render that which is due. If you ride along this little way, then you will soon come to this spring. It is colder than any other body of water, but still it boils more violently than any heating kettle. Above the spring hangs a basin, like gold, which is fastened to a chain and can be lowered into the spring. Beside the spring stands a stone pillar, and beside that a lovely little chapel. Now if you take the water with the basin and throw it on the stone, you will immediately get a violent storm. All the animals and birds which are in the vicinity will flee. Then you'll see lightning and hear thunder. Large trees will break off at the stump and there'll be heavy rain. If you manage to escape from there without injury, it may turn out better for you than for any other knight before.'

"Afterward I rode away in the direction he had indicated. At midday I saw the chapel and spreading over it a vine-tree, the most beautiful one growing on earth. I also saw where the basin was hanging, made of pure gold, and the chain as well. The spring was boiling so hard that it splashed in all directions, just like a hot spring, and yet it was ice-cold. The pillar was of the most beautiful emerald, with four red rubies beneath it. These shone with a redness like that of the rising sun when it glows in the east. I seized the basin rashly and filled it too full. I threw too much water on the pillar, because I immediately saw the sky become covered with dark clouds. More than sixty flashes of lightning at once struck my eyes. Out of the darkness of the clouds came snow, rain, and hail.

The storm was so terrible that it occurred to me a hundred times that I would probably not escape the lightning coming at me, or the large trees, and the violent gale, and that I would die. You can be sure that I was terrified then, completely deranged by fear, until the wind began to abate and the storm let up. God protected me and looked after me, for these tribulations lasted only a short while. Then the wind fell calm.

"When I saw that the earth was cleansed and the clouds had cleared from the sky, I rejoiced greatly. And if I have ever really experienced joy, then joy quickly causes one to forget care and drives away affliction. When the storm had broken, I saw in the vine-tree an enormous number of birds, so many that they covered all the branches of the tree. They sat so close together that I couldn't see the tree because of them. All of these birds sang so harmoniously that it seemed as if they had but one voice, and yet each was singing its own song, and no one sang another's song. I listened for a long time until they had finished the service which they were singing. I was comforted then by their joy. I have never heard such a beautiful song, and I don't believe anyone has, unless he went there to hear this one.

"I listened so long, and their song pleased me so much, that I was very foolish—as I later discovered—in remaining there as I did. Suddenly I heard a knight coming. He made such a clashing and clanging that I thought there were no fewer than ten. When I saw that he was all alone, I took my horse and weapons and mounted up. Immediately the other came rushing forward as fast as he could, like some one angry and ill-tempered.

"From as far off as I was able to see him he addressed me in a threatening tone: 'Ruffian, you have done me great disgrace and shame. If you had a charge to bring against me, you should have challenged me to a duel or asked me to make compensation in some other way—if I have indeed done you some wrong. But you have proceeded hostilely against me, who am innocent. You can be sure now, ruffian, that if I am able, you shall receive a most disgraceful share of great difficulties. Just see what damage you have done to my forest.

Rest assured, therefore, that you may expect neither peace
nor truce from me.'
    "When he had said this, we two met as quickly as our horses
could carry us. He was more than a head taller than I and
much stronger, and his horse was stronger than mine. So I
was really not well off trying to fight him. Now, even though I
was disgraced there, I shall nevertheless tell everything as it
happened. I thrust at his shield with all my might so that my
lance broke and the pieces straightway flew up over my head.
But he thrust me back off my horse with his sturdy lance so
that I lay on my back on the ground, disgraced and van-
quished. He took my horse and rode away with it. He did not
even deign to look back at me. So I remained sitting there,
shamed and disgraced, and didn't know what I should do. I
decided then to lay down my arms and go back to my host.
Shamefully I returned in the evening to his lodgings. He
came toward me immediately, friendly and cheerful, and wel-
comed me in the same manner as the evening before—and his
daughter as well. Every one in the hall talked about it, saying
that never before had a man gotten away from there—so far
as they knew—and not been slain or held in chains. Now I
have told you how foolishly I acted and what disgrace I
received from my journey."

CHAPTER 3

    "Heaven knows," said Sir Íven, "you are my close
kinsman, and you did not do well in concealing this from me
for so long. This I promise, if God permits, that I shall
avenge your disgrace."
    Then Kay answered: "Now, Íven, we can hear that you have
eaten well. You have more words than a full jug of wine. It is
said that a full cat is happy. Now it is after a meal, and you
wish to slay Sir Nodan.[3] Tell me, Sir Íven, whether you intend
to leave this evening or tomorrow for this duel. Be so kind,
sir, as to tell us, for we would like to accompany you. But now
I advise you—however it may turn out—wait first and see
what you dream tonight. I suspect that you may wish to
remain with us tomorrow."

Then the queen spoke: "Can it be that you are mad, Kay, that your tongue always speaks that which is evil and does not recognize that which is good? May your tongue be cursed since it can never keep silent about evil. You always mock men who are better than you. Every one who hears of you hates you because of your tongue. Your name will always be known for evil as long as the world remains."

"My lady," said Íven, "you should not exchange words with him, because every one can see that he always likes to mock strangers, and that he slanders his own comrades and brothers-in-arms."

At that moment the king came out of his quarters where he had been sleeping and asked what the discussion was about. The queen at once told him Kalebrant's whole story with great eloquence. When the king had heard this, he swore that within half a month he would leave with all his court and go to the spring, by Saint John's Eve at the latest.[4]

Íven then thought about his situation. If he went with the king, Kay would still mock him as before, and it was not certain that he would be granted the duel by the king. He decided that he should go away alone, and at once returned to his quarters. He asked his squire to get him his horse and his weapons and to take them secretly out to the city wall.

Sir Íven mounted his palfrey and rode all alone out of the place. The squire came after him and brought him his arms. Íven now mounted his horse and rode off alone until he found the castle of wood. There he received an even pleasanter reception than Kalebrant from the lord of the castle and the young lady. From there he rode into the forest to that black man who cared for the wild animals and bulls. The black man showed him the way to the spring. Íven immediately seized the basin and, filling it as full as possible, threw all the water onto the pillar. At once there arose a fierce wind and great torrents of rain and such a storm as was customary there. Afterward, when God had caused the storm to calm, the birds again settled on the vine-tree and sang joyously.

Before they had finished their song, the knight came riding with boiling anger and a great din, just as if he were driving a stag from the forest with his hounds. As soon as the two saw each other, they met with such great hatred, as if each had a

mortal offense to repay the other. Both had extremely strong,
stout lances. Their coats of mail cracked, their lances broke,
and the pieces flew up in the air. Then the two quickly drew
their swords and struck at each other, while protecting them-
selves with their shields. They fought with such great eager-
ness and ardor that the shields were split and fell to the
ground. They had so cut them into small pieces that it was no
longer possible to use them for protection. Then the swords
came down on shoulders and arms, on legs and loins. So
eagerly and bravely did they fight that neither gave ground to
the other. They sat as firmly as if they were stocks or stones.
Never did any one see two knights so eager to hasten the
other to his death. Neither wished to waste his blows, and they
paid such close attention to where they fell that their helmets
split and the rings of their coats of mail flew up in the air. It
was a wonder that such a hard and fierce battle should last so
long, but both were extremely courageous. Neither wished to
retreat an inch from the other, but each remained where he
was and awaited victory—or death. In one thing, however,
they behaved like courteous knights—neither wished to strike
or injure the other's horse. Both remained mounted the whole
time.

Finally Sir Iven cut into the knight's helmet with such a
great blow that his opponent acted as if he had lost his senses.
The knight was terrified because he had never before felt
such a blow. His helmet was cracked and his mail hood brok-
en. The sword had cut into his skull. When Íven pulled the
sword back, all the mail hood was covered with blood and brains.
The knight was certainly not to be reproached for fleeing
now, because he felt himself mortally wounded. There was no
use in defending himself any longer, and, recovering his
senses, he retreated as quickly as he could toward the castle.

The people in the castle saw their lord fleeing and im-
mediately had the bridge lowered and the fortress gate
opened. Like a falcon pursuing a crane, Sir Íven galloped at
full speed after the knight. Both were now riding as hard as
they could. Íven did all he could to overtake him, dead or
alive, because he knew Kay's scoffing and mockery. He was
sure that Kay would say he had never met the knight, if he

had no evidence of it. They now rode until they came to the knight's castle. Sir Íven pursued him through the streets of the city, where they met no one until they came to the knight's gateway. It was so narrow that not more than two could ride side by side at one time. Above the gateway a portcullis was drawn up. It was large, heavy, and sharp on the lower part, like a sword's edge, and it was set up like a crossbow. The minute anything touched it, no matter how little, down it came. When they got to the gateway, Sir Íven was so close to the knight that he could touch his saddlebow with his hand. At that moment the portcullis came rushing down and cut Íven's horse in two. It came so close to Íven that both his spurs were cut off by the blow, although it did not actually scratch him. But because of that he fell to the ground badly frightened.

A short distance away there was a large, sturdy gateway with a very stout door in it. The knight rode in through this gateway, which was then closed behind him. Thus Íven, distressed and distraught, was caught and locked in. The hall was shut off in all directions around him. The walls of this hall were all inlaid with pure gold and stained with wavy stains of every sort of color. Íven was most distressed, however, because he did not know which way the knight had gone or where he had gotten to. Now, a short distance from where he was, he saw a lovely girl, beautifully shaped, come out of a small room.

She immediately locked the door behind her, and when she perceived Sir Íven she began to speak to him, threateningly at first: "Good heavens, Sir Knight, I fear that you are not welcome here. If people find out about your presence here, they will cut you to pieces. My lord is critically wounded, and I know it is you who have slain him. My lady has suffered greatly, as have all her people. They are sitting with her now nearly bursting with sorrow. They all know that you are here in the hall, but because of that sorrow they are in no condition to seize you or slay you. But you are in their power, whenever they wish to seize you."

"Heaven knows that they shall never boast of that," Íven answered.

"That may prove true, if God permits," she replied, "because I shall help you as much as I can, since I think you are a valiant knight—you are not afraid, even though you have gotten into a terrible situation. I shall serve and honor you as best I can, because you once honored me at the court of King Arthur, when my lady had sent me there. You honored me more than all the others did. Although I was perhaps not as courteous as was fitting at court, you still were courteous toward me and assisted me, like a valiant man. I know that your name is Sir Íven and that you are the son of King Urien. Now I shall serve you and reward the courtesy which you showed me. Don't be afraid, you shall never be seized here, if you follow my advice. I have a certain ring which I intend to give you, although I want you to give it back to me when you are freed from here. The power of the stone in the ring is such that if the one who has it on his hand turns the stone toward his palm and closes his fist—then no mortal eyes can see that man."

Sir Íven thanked her for these words.

"Get up into this bed," she continued, "and sit there." She then brought him the best food and drink.

When he was full, he heard a great crying and shouting, that the lord of the castle was dead. The people began searching for the one who had killed him.

Then the girl returned to Sir Íven and said: "May God protect you. Do not leave this bed, and do not stir from here at all. You will see that those searching for you are going about like mad men and see nothing. That will be very entertaining for you, because you are not afraid to see them blind and mad. But now I must leave you for the time being."

CHAPTER 4

As soon as she had left, many men came into the hall with drawn swords. They thought they would avenge their lord because they saw the dead horse by the gate and believed the slayer was still in the hall. They went around searching but did not find him. They raised the gate which had done such harm to so many a man. Still they did not come upon him there. Then they returned to the hall and searched for him with terrible ferocity.

When they did not find him, they said: "What can be the reason for our not finding this man? Nothing living can get out of this hall, except a flying squirrel or a weasel, but now we find nothing left of him outside except his broken spurs." They went to search for him again. They searched throughout the whole hall, in beds and under footboards, but they did not come to the bed where he was.

At the same time the body of the knight was carried through the hall. Behind the body walked a lady so lovely that her equal was not to be found in all the world. She mourned and cried aloud with grief. At times she fell in a faint. All the people there were filled with sorrow. When the body was brought into the middle of the hall, all the wounds began to bleed, and the blood ran from the bier in all directions.[5]

Everyone then said: "That man who killed our lord is surely in here. Let us go and search for him again." But they did not find him this time any more than before, and when there no longer seemed to be any hope of finding him, they gave up the search.

The worthy lady, however, nearly burst from sorrow and cried: "If you, evil deceiver, are in here, you who slew my husband, come forward to me, if you are not a coward. Let me get my hands on you! I know that you have killed him through deceit, because in the whole world there was not his equal in bravery, accomplishments, and skill with weapons." So too, all those who were in the hall mourned and bewailed their lord. Then they carried him to church and buried him in the ground, and after that all went home.

A little later the girl returned to Sir Íven. He welcomed her and said: "Please, could you make it possible for me to see that lady who was walking through the hall?"

The girl showed him a window in the hall from which he could see where the lady of the castle was sitting, mourning her husband. It was the greatest sorrow for Sir Íven that he could not speak with her. She wailed and mourned. At times she fell in a faint, at times she choked herself and wanted to kill herself. She was as fair as the dawn, her color as if the snow-white lily and the red rose had been mingled together, and her hair as if it contained gold. Her eyes shone like those stones which people call *carbunculi*. Íven wished to see her all the more and loved her with all his heart. He wanted very much to speak to her. So great was his love for her that he wished to die there rather than not speak to her at all, or at least try to win her love.

At that moment the young lady who was taking care of him returned and saw him musing and in the bonds of love, as if he did not know what he wanted. She asked him: "Sir Íven, what is it that dwells inside you now?"

"That mood which pleases me greatly," he replied.

"For Heaven's sake," she said, "do not conceal the truth from me. How can one be pleased when his enemies are looking for him and wish to kill him—unless he desires death rather than life?"

"God knows, young lady," he said, "I certainly do not desire my death, but what I have seen does please me and will continue to do so as long as I live."

"I understand very well the direction your words are taking," she replied, "but I can get you away at once, if you wish to leave."

"I would rather die than leave during these seven days," he answered.[6]

Then the girl said: "You shall go into my little room and wait there until I am able to accomplish what I see to be your greatest desire." And she looked after all his needs.

CHAPTER 5

The girl was not afraid to say whatever she wanted to her lady because she was her teacher and counselor. She went to her now and said: "Your conduct seems strange to me. Do you think that through this sorrow you torment yourself with you can bring back your lord—who is dead?"

"No," the lady replied, "that's not the way it is; but still it is

better to die of sorrow and grief—and thus follow my hus-
band—than to live."

The girl spoke: "May God never let that be so. May he
rather give you an equally good, equally brave, and equally
mighty husband, because nothing is impossible with God."

The lady said: "Never have you told such a lie, because
never before was his equal born on this earth."

"Oh yes, there was," the girl replied, "and a much better
one, if you would dare to marry him."

"Be silent and go away," the lady commanded.

But the girl asked: "Who will defend your kingdom when
King Arthur comes next week to the spring and the stone
pillar? Stop crying and consider your honor! There is no
knight with you who will dare to split a shield or break a lance
or charge against the least of his knights, when King Arthur
comes here with his army. You and all your kingdom will be
in his power then."

Now the lady perceived that the girl was giving her good
advice, but she had that habit—as do other women—of deny-
ing what is on their minds and forsaking what they want most
to have. "Go away," she said, "and don't mention such things
again, or you'll pay for it. You talk so much that your words
make me angry."

"My lady," the girl said, "may God bless you. Now it is clear
that you are a woman and have a woman's temper. When they
are offered something good or are given good advice, they
shun it and hide themselves."

After that the girl went away, while the lady remained
sitting there. She pondered what had been said and perceived
that the girl was more in the right. The lady wanted very
much to know where that knight could be found who might
be as good as her knight, or perhaps even better. But
although she wanted badly to find this out, still she had for-
bidden her to mention the matter again.

The girl then spoke:[7] "Is it nice, my lady, that you destroy
yourself with grief and sorrow? Spare yourself; it isn't fitting
for you, so worthy a lady, to torment yourself with such long
sorrow and sadness. Consider your honor and your own
particular womanly qualities—and the defense of your king-

dom. Do you really think that all valor, courage, and accomplishments died with your husband? An equally good or even better knight can still be found in this world."

"You lie," the lady said, "but nevertheless name him to me, the one who is as valiant as my lord was."

"If I give you good advice and tell you the truth," the girl replied, "you will be displeased and angry with me."

"No," said the lady, "that I won't."

The girl continued then: "Now if two knights arm themselves for battle and meet one another, and if one attacks but the other wins, which of them do you think is the better?"

"The one who wins seems to me better than the other who is vanquished," the lady replied.

"Now you judge correctly," said the girl, "the one who overcame your husband and pursued him into the courtyard here is the more valiant."

"You always speak evil and foolishness!" the lady cried, "You must be filled with an evil spirit. Get out as quickly as possible and never come into my sight again to bring up such words."

"My lady," the girl replied, "I just knew that I would earn your displeasure if I gave you good advice and looked out for your needs." Then she left and went back to Sir Íven and waited upon him as usual. The lady remained sitting there and thought about what the girl had said. She saw that she had given her good advice and that she had been wrong in reproaching her.

The next morning, when the girl returned, the lady addressed her: "Dear girl, I ask you to forgive me for what I said to you so harshly yesterday. I now wish to follow your advice. Tell me what you know about this knight whom you have talked about so much to me. What sort of a man is he? What is his family? Is he so well-bred and of such a powerful family that he befits me? If so, then I am willing to promise you that I will make him lord of myself and of all my kingdom. But still, this will have to be done in such a way that people will not slander and reproach me and say 'This is the woman who married him who killed her husband.'"

The girl answered: "You needn't fear that, for he is in all

respects the most valiant man who has come from the line of Abel."

"What is his name?" asked the lady.

"Sir Íven," the girl replied.

"Heaven knows," said the lady, "I have heard that he is a most valiant and courteous knight and the son of King Urien. When can I see him?"

"At the end of seven days," the girl answered.

"That's all too long," the lady said, "can't I see him to-morrow?"

"It's perfectly clear," replied the girl, "even if he were a bird, he couldn't make it here that quickly."

"Seven days will be too late," the lady said.

The girl answered: "I'll send for him so that he will come here at the end of three days. During this period it is fitting that you call your men together and ask them for advice about the king who is on his way here. Ask them who is available to preserve your custom, and see whether they advise upholding it and defending your spring. Tell them also that a famous knight of good family wishes to marry you and is offering you his defense. You are willing to accept that offer with their consent. I know their cowardice; not one of them will dare to take the matter up. They will all agree to your wish."

Then the lady spoke: "By my faith, that's the way I had intended it should be. I am willing to agree to that, and so it shall be. Go quickly now and do not delay any longer. Arrange for him to be in your charge as soon as possible, and I shall gather my men together." Thus they ended their discussion.

CHAPTER 6

Now the girl pretended to her lady that she had sent for Sir Íven. Every day she prepared a bath for him, washed and combed him. She also prepared a rich suit of clothes for him, made of new scarlet material and adorned with a gold brooch set with precious jewels, and a belt with a

special goldwork, made with much skill. There was a belt-
purse, woven with gold with as many kinds of fine workman-
ship as women's handicraft is capable of. Thus, she dressed
Sir Íven nobly and fittingly in every respect. Then she went to
her lady and told her that her messenger had returned and
had accomplished his errand—everything that she had desired
—like an intelligent fellow.

"When will Íven come here?" asked the lady.

"My lady," the girl answered, "he has already arrived and is
in my care."

"Let him come here as quickly as possible," the lady said,
"but in secrecy, while no one is near us. Watch carefully that
no others come here."

At that the girl went to see Sir Íven but did not reveal to
him by her look the joy of her heart and mind. She said:
"Now my lady is fully informed about my having concealed
you. It's no use for you to conceal yourself any longer,
because she now knows everything that has happened. She
rebukes me severely and makes many charges against me.
Nevertheless, she has made peace between us, and you are to
come with me now to her. She will not wrong you nor distress
you. Don't be afraid on that account, if only because it does
not befit me to lie to you or deceive you. My lady wishes to
have you as a captive in her power, so completely that neither
your head nor your heart can escape."

"Heaven knows," Íven replied, "that can't distress me, since
that is what I desire very much. For her I am certainly willing
to be a captive."

"Follow me then," she said, "and don't be afraid. Don't
think about the possibility of being harmed here."

Thus she threatened him, but afterward she reassured him
concerning his desire. It is possible that she talked about the
"captive of love" and declared that he was "captive," for
everyone who loves greatly is a captive. The girl now led Sir
Íven to that place which would please him. He feared that he
might be deceived—which is not strange since he did not have
any expectation of being granted security.

When they entered, the lady was sitting on a red silk quilt.
She said nothing upon their entrance, even though she was

very eager to see Íven. He stopped then and stood at some distance from her.

The girl spoke: "Woe be to you and that constraint which prevails in the quarters of a powerful lady, but woe also to that knight who has neither speech nor wit, tongue nor mouth." Then she addressed Íven: "Come here and sit beside my lady. Don't be afraid that she will bite you. Ask her, rather, for peace and reconciliation. I shall help you and plead along with you that she forgive you the destruction and death of her husband, Sodal the Red."[8]

Sir Íven immediately clasped his hands together, fell to his knees, and said: "My lady, I do not intend to ask for mercy. Instead, I wish to thank you for whatever you desire to do with me, because that will never displease me."

"Indeed," the lady said, "and what do you gain if I wish to have you killed?"

"My lady, may God thank you; never shall I say anything else but that *you* decide."

"I have never seen a man before," she replied, "who submitted so completely to my courtly ways and womanhood. I have not compelled you to do that."

"My lady," he said, "there is no compulsion as powerful as that which compels me to do this—to obey you in everything you wish to ask of me. I shall gladly do everything that is pleasing to you, and I am not afraid, even if the greatest danger is involved. If I might compensate for the death of the one I killed—I did not transgress against him[9]—then I would do that so well that no one might find fault with it."

"Tell me now," the lady said, "and free yourself of all calumny, didn't you transgress greatly against me when you killed my lord and husband?"

"My lady," said Íven, "may God thank you. If your lord attacked me, how did I transgress when I defended myself? If some one wishes to destroy or kill another, and if the latter in defending himself kills the other, tell me if he transgresses at all in doing that."

"No," she answered, "no one can say that truthfully. For that reason I know it would not improve my affairs to have had you killed. But I would like to know what force it is that compels you so. Where does such benevolence come from that you are willing to obey me so completely and do my will? Everything which I complained of and in which you transgressed against me shall be forgiven. Sit down now beside me here and tell me how it happens that you are so well-disposed toward me."

"My heart compels me to such a desire," he said.

"What is the cause?" she asked.

"That beloved beauty of yours," he answered.

"How has beauty transgressed against you?" she asked.

"My lady," he answered, "by making me love."

"Whom?"

"You yourself, my dear lady."

"Indeed," she said, "in what way?"

"With such great ardor," he said, "that in no way could it be greater; whatever I do, my heart dwells completely with you. So much do I love you that I desire never to be in a different place, and it would please me both to live and to die with you."

"Do you dare to defend my spring for the sake of me?" she asked.

"Yes, as God knows," he replied, "against any mortal man."

"Know then, truly," she said, "that we two are reconciled in all those matters which please you."

In this manner they became reconciled. The lady had earlier held a meeting with her men, and now she said: "Let us go from here into the hall where my men await us. They have advised me to marry because of our great need, since they now see what is at stake. So I am willing to do as they advised. Now I give myself to you, for it is not fitting for me to refuse the offer of a good knight and a king's son."

CHAPTER 7

Now the girl had accomplished all that she desired. The lovely lady led Sir Íven into the hall, which was filled with knights and powerful chieftains. Íven was such an extremely handsome man that all those who were sitting in the hall marveled at him, his gallant stature and noble appearance. All stood up and greeted him with bows, saying among themselves: "So this is the worthy lord who is going to marry our lady. Woe to anyone who is displeased by that; he certainly appears blessed by fortune. Heaven knows, the sovereign queen of Rome could fittingly marry such a worthy man. It would now be more fitting that they had clasped their hands together."[10] Thus spoke all those who were in the hall.

Thereupon the lovely lady sat down in the highest seat of the hall so that she could look out over everyone and everyone could look upon her. Sir Íven, out of humility and to show her honor, said that he wished to sit at her feet. However, she took him by his right hand and seated him beside her in the highest seat. After that she called upon her steward and asked him to make known his counsel so that all might hear it.

He was very eloquent and knowledgeable and spoke loudly enough that all who were in the hall heard his words: "My lords, it is fitting for us to be on our guard against difficulties and to plan to defend ourselves against hostilities and foes, because those injuries which one wards off and guards against will do less harm than those which come upon one unawares. Every day King Arthur has been making preparation for his journey here with a great host of chosen knights to lay waste to our property. Our lady now seeks advice from all of you as to whether she should marry. Scarcely seven days have passed since she lost her husband, and that is a truly great sorrow for her, but a woman cannot be a knight or bear arms. Now she *must* have a valiant knight; never before has her need been so great. All of you, advise her well, now, that she provide herself and us with a lord and chieftain, rather than let that custom which has been upheld here for more than sixty years be lost."

When he had said this, all answered in agreement that it was most fitting for their lady to marry. All went and knelt before her and asked her to accept and observe that advice which they, her firmest friends, offered. She made them go on asking for quite some time, as if she were not inclined to do what actually was more pleasing to her than to any of

them. Indeed, she would have exercised her will, even if all of
them had spoken against it, for it is the custom of most
women—and a natural characteristic—to effect that which lies
uppermost in their hearts and is truly pleasing to them,
whether or not it is beneficial for them. For that reason it is
difficult for many to guard against the fickleness of women.

The lady now spoke: "Good sirs, the excellent knight who is
sitting here beside me has asked for my hand in marriage. I
have heard much good concerning his renowned conduct and
actions. He is the son of King Urien and a most valiant
knight, nobler even than befits me. His name is Sir Íven, of
whom you have often heard good reports."

Then they all arose and again fell on their knees before her
and begged her for a long time to marry Sir Íven. She finally
agreed, pretending that she was acceding to their request,
although she would have done so even if it had displeased all
of them. Sir Íven then arose and betrothed himself to the
lady. She, in turn, gave herself into his keeping, with all her
duchy which Laudun, her father, had possessed—he had been
one of the most famous chieftains in England. Some of the
finest songs which the Welsh and Britons sing are composed
about him. Bishops and barons, earls and knights were now
invited to come there, and the wedding was celebrated with all
honors, great pomp, and abundant provisions. It lasted until
Saint John's Eve. Everyone did honor and reverence to Sir
Íven now and forgot the one who was dead.

CHAPTER 8

Now the story turns to King Arthur who had been
making preparations for the departure. So many of his
knights were eager to go with him to see those marvels of
which they had heard concerning the spring and the stone
pillar that no one remained behind. The king set up his tents
around the spring, and when he was sitting in his tent, Kay
began to speak: "I don't see Sir Íven here, although when he
was drunk with wine he said that he would avenge his kins-
man. Now everyone can see he has fled. He was certainly
foolish to bring upon himself the accusation of boasting."

Sir Gawain then answered: "There you're reproaching a better man than you. You should be disgraced because of your words—and so you shall be, if you don't keep quiet."

"I won't mention him again today, now that I see it displeases you," Kay replied.

The king now took the gold basin, filled it with as much water as he could, and threw it over the pillar. Immediately it rained and hailed; there were flashes of lightning and terrible claps of thunder, and a violent gale. When it abated, Sir Íven came charging into the forest, well armed and on a good charger, both strong and bold. Kay saw this and asked the king for permission to ride against this man in single combat. When Kay received the king's permission, he at once mounted his charger fully armed and rode at Sir Íven with great ferocity. Each came at the other. Íven recognized Kay by his armor. When they met, each thrust at the other, but the shaft of Kay's lance broke to pieces, and Íven knocked him far back off his horse. Kay landed head downward with his feet in the air; his helmet stuck fast in the mud, so that he had great difficulty getting his head out. He now turned on his belly but did not dare stand up. Taking Kay's horse, Sir Íven was unwilling to do anything more to him.

Íven then rode to the king and spoke: "My lord, have this horse looked after, because I would do you too much wrong if I in any way intended to keep that which touches upon your honor."[11]

"What sort of person are you?" the king replied. "I am unable to recognize you—unless I hear your name."

"My lord, my name is Íven."

Now Kay lay there, disgraced and distressed, shamed and vanquished—and dealt with as he deserved, because he had said that Sir Íven would not dare to wait for him. Everyone else rejoiced at Kay's mishap, since he had no friends at the king's court. The king himself also made fun of him, for Kay had brought his disgrace upon himself—of his own free will, without anyone's urging. Sir Gawain was the happiest of all, because he was fond of Íven above all other knights. With many fair words the king now asked Sir Íven to tell him how he came to be there. Íven related all the events, how he had slain the knight and married the lovely lady, and he invited

King Arthur home to a banquet. The king accepted the invitation gladly. Sir Íven sent one of the king's squires to announce their coming in advance so that quarters and the halls might be made ready.

As soon as the lady heard this, she had the whole castle prepared and hung with costly materials. She sent five hundred knights out to meet the king, who was then conducted into the castle with all honor. The lady herself went to meet the king. She intended to hold his stirrup herself while he dismounted, but the king dismounted before she could do so and went to meet her. He kissed her, and they exchanged tender embraces. And so she led the king into the castle. The king was ushered into the loveliest hall of the castle. Courtly maidens went out to receive the king's knights. The young lady Luneta, who had helped Sir Íven, approached Sir Gawain, kissed him, and led him to his quarters. They talked together, and she told him all about how she had helped Sir Íven. Their conversation ended with them promising love to each other; she was to be his lady. The king remained at the feast for seven days. When Arthur was preparing to leave, Sir Gawain told Íven that he ought to go along with the king and not remain in the castle any longer. If he remained there and immediately entered into a life of ease, he might ruin his knightly reputation and accomplishments. Gawain was able to convince Íven, so that he agreed to accompany him, provided he got leave from his lady.

Íven now went to her and said: "My most lovely lady, you are my life and heart, my body's comfort, well-being, and joy. Grant me one request which I ask of you, which will be to my fame and the honor of both of us."

She immediately answered: "Whatever pleases you and you wish to ask of me, all that shall be as you desire, for you are my lord."

Then Íven said: "I ask that you permit me to accompany King Arthur and take part in tournaments with his knights so that they will not consider me more a coward now than before."

"I will permit you to do this on one condition," she replied, "that you return no later than at the end of twelve months. If, however, you fail to do so, if you forsake me and break your oath, then you shall forfeit all my love and friendship all the rest of your life. You shall be dishonored among all those valiant men who honorably take a wife for themselves—if you are not here with me then."

Íven said with a deep sigh: "You have set too long a time for our meeting, because I will always be wanting to see you as quickly as possible. But there can be hindrances which prevent me—if I am sick, or wounded, or captured."

"My lord," she said, "I shall see to it that you will not be hindered thus. Put this ring, which I am lending you, on your finger now. It has such power that if one is wearing this stone, he cannot be captured, weapons will not cut him, and he will suffer no wounds or other misfortunes. Never before have I been willing to loan this ring to any knight."

After that Íven took leave of his lady, as did King Arthur. Sir Íven and his lady parted with great sorrow. Íven and Gawain now rode off, and there was not a single knight who could stand against Sir Íven. Twelve months passed in this manner, in fact nearly a year and a half. Every one honored him and served him. Then one time the sister of the earl gave a great banquet, and King Arthur was invited there with all his best knights.[12] Sir Gawain and Sir Íven, returning from a tournament, also came there and pitched their tents outside the stronghold. When the king found that out, he rode out to welcome them and sat down together with them. After the king had been sitting there a little while, it occurred to Íven that the period had elapsed which his lady had set for him. He was now so filled with remorse that he nearly went out of his mind, and he felt great shame before other knights.

CHAPTER 9

As Íven sat sorrowfully thinking about this matter, a young lady came riding to the tent. She dismounted at once and, throwing off her cloak, entered the tent and came before the king. She greeted him and Sir Gawain and all the knights who were there—except Íven—and brought them the greetings of her lady. But Íven she called a real traitor, a liar, and a deceiver. She said it was very obvious that he claimed to be unwavering in the fidelity of his love, faithful in his pledges, and truthful in his words—"but you are a guileful, treacherous person and a thief. My lady thought that you were sincere; it never entered her mind that you would steal her love and betray her. You, Íven, have slain my lady, because she has lain in her bedroom filled with sorrow and anxiety, getting no rest either by day or by night since the twelve months have passed when you promised her to return—and eight days more. Now she sends you this message: you are to send back her ring and never visit her again."

Sir Íven was silent, not knowing what to say; he had lost both speech and wit. Rushing at him, the girl seized the ring from him. She then wished the king good health and commended him to God, along with all his men—except Íven alone.

Íven was very distressed now and wanted to go somewhere where no one knew him. He hated nothing as much as himself. Such a great madness came over him then that he wanted to take vengeance upon himself, for he had now lost all comfort. The others let him go off all alone because he had no wish to be comforted by their words. He rushed out of the tent and into the forest. He had lost nearly all his reason and tore off his clothes. When he had been running for a long time, he met a boy who was carrying a bow and five arrows. Íven took the bow and arrows from the boy, then went rushing on in the forest. He shot animals for himself and ate the meat raw. When he had run through the forest for a long time, he came upon the house of a hermit. But when the hermit saw him, he perceived that Íven did not have full possession of his senses. The hermit gave him bread and water, because he was afraid of him, and directed him to be on his way. He prayed to God that he would never return. Íven ate the bread, even though it was poorly baked; it was soggy and full of bran. Íven had never eaten worse bread. As soon as he was full, he ran back into the forest. He was very mindful of the good the hermit had done him, however, and not a day passed without him bringing in some animal. The good man prepared it for him and also gave him water to drink.

One day, after Íven had been living this way for a long time, he lay sleeping in the forest. Three girls who were riding through the forest, accompanying their lady, found him lying there. When they saw him asleep, one of them got off her horse and went over to where he lay. She observed him for a long time before she recognized him, since he now appeared very different from the way he had been before. Finally she recognized him from a scar on his face, and it all seemed very strange to her. She mounted her horse and rode weeping back to her lady.

"My lady," she said, "I have found Sir Íven, the most excellent knight who has ever borne arms. I don't know for what misdeed so valiant a fellow is in such a serious state. I suspect that he has suffered a great sorrow and lost his reason because of it. Otherwise, if he had his full senses, he would not behave this way. It would be much better if he now had his full reason—the way he was when he was at his height— and if he would be willing to stay with you and help you, since Earl Alies has done great damage to you in those hostile acts which he has committed. If this man were to receive help and recovered his health, he would quickly drive away your enemies."

"Never fear," the lady answered, "with God's help we two shall certainly rid his head and heart of that raging storm of madness which torments him—unless he runs away. Let's hurry home now, for it occurs to me that I have an ointment which Morgan the Wise gave me. She told me that neither frenzy nor foolishness would ever destroy the head or heart of the person who was rubbed with that ointment."

They started off for the castle at once as quickly as possible. The lady took the box which contained the ointment, gave it to the girl, and told her with a stern warning not to be too generous with the ointment. She was to rub his head and neck but nothing else. The lady also gave her a new suit of clothes of scarlet and the finest linens. The girl took two horses with her, a very fine charger and a gentle palfrey. When she came into the forest, she tethered the horses, went to where Íven was sleeping, and rubbed his head and neck, and his whole trunk as well, with the ointment until it was completely gone from the box. Then she left him lying asleep in the hot sunshine, so the ointment dried on him. She placed the suit of clothes beside him before she went away. When she had not gone very far from him, she stopped under a tree, since she wanted to see what he would do.

A little while later Íven woke up and had recovered his reason. He saw that he was swarthy and sunburnt, naked and disgraced, but he did not know what the cause of that was. He saw a new suit of clothes lying beside him and decided to get dressed. When he had dressed and wanted to leave, he found that he had become so weak that he could not walk and only barely stand. Then he saw where the girl was sitting on a palfrey with another horse on a lead. The girl rode toward him now, and, acting as if she did not recognize him, she asked his name.

"I beg you not to inquire about my name," Íven replied, "but please lend or give me that horse which is following you on a lead."

"I'll gladly give you this palfrey," she answered, "but you must follow me to the castle of my lady."

Íven mounted the palfrey, and they now both rode to the castle and to the hall of the lady. The lady came forward at once and received him with great joy and hospitality. He now enjoyed with them a life easy in all respects—everything that he wished for. He stayed there for six weeks; at the end of this time he had gotten back all his strength.

CHAPTER 10

At that time Earl Alies was attacking the castle and the rest of the lady's kingdom. He was in the process of burning a village which was near the castle. Sir Íven saw this and asked the lady to call out her army against the earl. He requested for himself such weapons as he might choose from among those in the castle. Then he armed himself quickly, jumped on a magnificent steed, and rode out of the castle with the whole army.

As soon as they met, Íven thrust his lance through a knight
and hurled him to the ground dead. In that charge he killed
ten knights. Those who were following him now grew bold at
the sight of his valor and chivalry and, riding forward boldly,
fought well. At this time the lovely lady went up into the
battlements of the castle, accompanied by many of her people,
in order to watch the struggle.

"See," said those who were in the castle, "how this knight
proves himself all alone before the rest, and how his armor is
completely stained with the blood of the ones he has killed.
See how he rides through their host!"

Íven's shield was so completely cut to pieces that nothing
was left. Upon each of those who struck any blow at him he
took vengeance so swiftly and valiantly that no one was eager
to strike at him again. He lulled his opponents into such a
deep sleep that none of their companions were able to awaken
them. When his shield had become useless to him, he still
broke lance after lance on his enemies so that it amounted to
a good ninety before evening came. What he accomplished
with his lances meant great destruction of life for his enemies.
Between the time that he broke one lance and got another, he
used his sword.

When the young ladies of the castle saw him in battle and
perceived that he was such an extraordinarily valiant knight,
they said: "That woman would be fortunate to whom such a
magnificent knight gave his love. He is so powerful in the
exchange of blows that no knight is his match. He is as
outstanding above other knights as a wax candle is above
tallow candles, or a sunbeam above moonlight. No knight is as
harsh as a lion against his enemies, but as gentle as a lamb
toward his own men, the way he is. May God grant that he be
our and our lady's lord and rule all the kingdom."

The earl took to flight then, along with all those of his host
who still remained alive. Sir Íven and his knights pursued the
fleeing host and slew their enemies. Because of Íven his men
were as fearless and resolute as if a stone wall stood around
them for protection. The earl fled, but Íven pursued him
until they came onto a steep path a short distance from the
castle. There they stopped. Sir Íven seized him, raised his

sword, and intended to kill him. Asking for quarter, the earl surrendered himself into Íven's power, because he could neither defend himself nor escape. After that Íven led the captive earl behind him and handed him over to his enemies, who were then consoled and rejoiced greatly. The lady of the castle rode out to meet them with many men and women and welcomed Sir Íven. He handed over to her the earl, who pledged her his fidelity—to do everything she might find pleasing. To ensure that, he provided her with guarantors and pledged solemnly that she and all her kingdom would in the future be safe from him and from all those whom he commanded. And he would repay her for all the damages which she might claim.

Now that everything was specified concerning the treaty between the two in a manner satisfactory to the lady, Sir Íven took leave to depart. He did not at all wish to remain there any longer. He left so quickly that there was no possibility of dissuading him, and he allowed no one to accompany him. He returned to the road by which he had come. The lovely lady was left sitting there, angry and sorrowful because he did not wish to stay there. She had wanted to show him honor and make him the lord of all her possessions, if that had pleased him.

Sir Íven now rode until he entered a deep valley and a dense forest. Suddenly he heard noises and a distressing cry. He immediately headed in the direction of the sounds. In a clearing he saw a big lion and a serpent holding onto its tail and burning it with poison and fire which it blew on it. The lion's loins were singed from the serpent's poison and fire. When Sir Íven saw this strange event, he pondered which one of them he should assist. He dismounted and tied his horse so that the serpent would not harm it. He drew his sword and covered himself with his shield so that the fire which the serpent was blowing would not injure him. Its jaws were as big as the mouth of a furnace. In whatever manner he and the lion might deal with each other afterward, Íven still wanted to help it now, because he perceived that the lion was calling on him for help. He cut the serpent in two in the middle and then into small pieces. When the lion got loose, Íven thought

it would rush at him; he prepared to defend himself. How-
ever, the lion immediately crawled toward him, turned its
belly up, and wet its muzzle with tears, as if it wished to ask
for peace. Thus it placed itself in Sir Íven's power. He
received it joyfully and thanked God that He had sent him
such a companion. Íven now rode on his way, while the lion
ran along in front of him. They stayed in the forest for half a
month, and the lion hunted deer for food for them.

Now Íven rode past a tall vine-tree. Under it he saw the
spring, which was mentioned earlier, and the chapel and
recognized the pillar. At once such a great madness came over
him that he nearly fell unconscious. His sword, which he had
recently sharpened, fell from its sheath, and in his madness
and convulsions he wounded himself both on the neck and
under the nipples. As soon as the lion saw that, it took the
sword in its teeth, dragged it away from Íven, and set it in a
tree stump so that it stuck firmly. Then the lion ran around
Íven and, thinking him dead, intended to kill itself. No one
has ever heard worse sounds than it made, because it thought
it had lost its master for good. At that Íven recovered his
senses, and when the lion saw that, it stopped. Sir Íven
bemoaned his folly at having broken his faith with the lady.

He cried out very sorrowfully: "To what purpose should I,
wretched man, live, I who have been so heedless? What
should I do but kill myself? I have lost my joy and consolation
and by my own misdeed turned my reputation into remorse,
my honor into annihilation, my delight into depression, my
life into loathing, my heart into anxiety, my sweetheart into an
enemy, and my freedom into outlawry. Why do I delay any
longer in killing myself?"

A wretched woman who was locked up in the chapel heard
this and, calling to him, asked who he was. But he asked her
who she was and why she was there.

"I am a wretch," she replied, "so wretched that nothing
living is more dejected or distressed than I."

"Be silent," Íven said, "*your* sorrow is consolation compared
to mine."

"How can that be," she asked, "since you are free to go
anywhere you wish, but I am captured and locked up, and my

fate has been decreed—tomorrow I shall die because of the evil doings of those who hate me. They accuse me of treachery, but I have done nothing to deserve those charges. Unless I find some one who would defend me against them, tomorrow they will burn me at the stake or hang me like a thief."

"Now first of all," said Íven, "I can prove that I have greater sorrow than you, because you can be rescued, but I can not."

"No," she said, "I can not be rescued, because there are only two knights in this world who dare to fight alone against three."

"Why does one knight have to fight alone against three?" asked Íven.

"Because those three accuse me of treachery."

"Who," Íven asked, "are the two knights who are willing to do so much for your sake?"

"They are Sir Gawain and Sir Íven—it is because of him, Sir Íven, that I, who am innocent, must die tomorrow."

"If you are the young lady I think you are—Luneta who saved my life in the castle of my lady—then you are not going to die tomorrow. If you are she, then I am Íven. But who are the ones making this charge of treachery against you?"

"I am certainly the one who helped you when you were in distress," she answered, "and I was responsible for my lady wanting to marry you. So when you violated the appointed day, she got angry with me and placed a charge against me. Her steward had been continually stealing her property, and when he now found out that he could get vengeance on me—he hated me with all his evil heart because I knew of his misconduct, as my lady had told me earlier—he wanted to have me killed on account of the treachery which he accused me of having committed against my lady in the union of you two. No one spoke in my defense except I alone. So it finally came about that a period of half a year was set for me in which to get some knight who was willing to rescue me by fighting alone against these three, who are the bravest in my lady's court. I have ridden to the court of King Arthur but found no one there who was willing to help me, because some knight has taken the queen away, and Sir Gawain was off

riding in search of her. No one could give me any informa-
tion about Sir Íven."

"My dear," Íven then said, "rest assured that I shall rescue
you tomorow—or else die."

CHAPTER 11

Afterward Sir Íven rode away to find quarters for
the night, and his lion followed him. When he had ridden for
a short time, he came out of the forest and saw a large, sturdy
castle. However, the whole surrounding district was so com-
pletely laid waste that there was not even a hut left. As Íven
rode toward the castle, the drawbridge was lowered at once,
and he rode in. The people were afraid of him because of the
animal but nevertheless bade him welcome there. They
wanted him to tie the animal up, but he said it would do them
no injury and rode to the hall. Knights and courtly young
ladies came and welcomed him with a great show of friend-
liness, but as soon as the crowd dispersed, those who re-
mained were filled with grief and sorrow. This seemed
strange to Íven who asked the master of the house what the
matter was.

"I would like to tell you," the lord of the castle said, "if I
knew that it would not distress you."

"How can it distress me?" Íven inquired, "I ask you to tell
me."

"A giant has done me great harm," the lord of the castle
answered, "and he wants me to give him my daughter, who is
the most beautiful of all girls. The giant's name is Fjalls-
harfir.[13] I had six sons, the handsomest men and most valiant
knights. He has killed two before my eyes and intends to kill
four tomorrow, unless I give him my daughter in marriage.
He has also laid waste all the land around here."

When Sir Íven had heard all this, he said: "Why don't you
send men or go yourself to the court of the most courteous
King Arthur to seek help there? There is always some one at
his court who will dare to fight against the giant."

"I would long since have had enough help, if Sir Gawain

had been at court," said the master of the house, "because my wife is his sister by the same parents. But a knight came to the king's court and took the queen away, because she was in the keeping of Kay. Sir Gawain has gone off in search of them. Surely, she was foolish when she gave herself into the keeping of such a knight."

When Íven had heard his lament, he said: "I will gladly expose myself to this danger tomorrow for the sake of your sons and daughter—on provision that it does not delay me too long, for I have given my pledge to be somewhere else at midday."

The master of the house thanked him warmly for his good intent and immediately sent for his wife and daughter to tell them that a knight had come there who was willing to fight against the giant. At that moment a young lady, his daughter, came up, accompanied by his wife; they were both very lovely. The two women came at once to Íven and wanted to throw themselves at his feet, but he sprang up and begged them not to, saying that he intended to help them for the sake of Sir Gawain. Íven remained with them during the evening and enjoyed great hospitality. Every one was happy now and full of confidence that he would deliver their castle because of his valor and his companion, the lion, which accompanied him. Later he went to sleep.

In the morning, when it was barely light, they saw the giant approaching the castle. He had a large iron club on his shoulder and a whip in his hand. Before him he drove four knights, the sons of the duke of the castle, and struck them as often as possible. They were weak and thin and without clothing. A fat, bloated dwarf led them, while the giant walked behind and beat them with his whip.

The giant now shouted at the lord of the castle: "I'll kill your sons at once before your eyes, unless you give me your daughter."

When Sir Íven heard this, he armed himself and rode boldly out of the castle toward the giant. All the people in the castle prayed that God would protect the knight against this monster. The giant, who was a sight to inspire terror, immediately rushed at him, but Íven in turn charged boldly and thrust his lance into the giant's chest so that blood gushed out at once. At that moment the giant struck at Íven with his iron club, but then God shielded him so that the blow did not hit the knight. When the lion saw that the giant intended to harm its master, it leaped up onto the giant's shoulder, bit his neck, and tore the flesh off all the way down to his loins. As the giant started to turn on the lion, Íven struck him on the shoulder so that the arm flew off and the iron club fell down. He immediately struck a second blow at the neck, and the head flew off. The giant tumbled to the ground then with such a great crash that all the earth in the vicinity shook. All the people in the castle saw this. They and the duke at once rushed out to meet Íven, placed themselves and the castle in his power and asked him to remain with them. Íven replied that he was unable to do that. The duke then offered him his sons and daughter as companions.

Íven refused that and said: "If you have any desire to do what I wish, then send your four sons and daughter together with this dwarf to Sir Gawain, when you learn that he has come back to the court of King Arthur."

"My lord," said the duke, "I ask you to tell me your name."

"Not just at present," Íven answered.

"What are we to tell Sir Gawain, then?" asked the duke.

"Say that I am called the Knight of the Lion, and that I am very well known to him, and he to me. If you find Sir Gawain, tell him nothing more. Now we must part. What distresses me most is that I have stayed here too long, because before midday has passed I will have enough to do in another place—if I get there in time."

CHAPTER 12

Now Sir Íven rode as hotly as he could until he came to the chapel. There he saw a great pyre laid and the girl bound both hand and foot. She had no clothes on except a nightshirt and was about to be thrown onto the pyre. A large crowd of people had gathered there. Íven charged fiercely into the midst of the crowd; a space was opened for him at once. Rushing to the pyre, he cut the bonds off the girl and asked where the one was who had placed the charges against her—"I have come now to defend your case."

"My lord," the girl answered, "if you had been a bit later in coming, I would quickly have been fire and ashes. May God grant you strength and power to such a degree as I know that I am innocent of those charges which they have made against me."

Then the steward and his two brothers spoke: "You know how to tell big lies! Anyone who thinks your vows and pretty talk are true is in a bad way. He who is willing to die for you here will be taking a great burden upon himself. There's one of him but three of us, and I advise him to be gone as quickly as possible, before more happens."

"Let him who is afraid flee!" Sir Íven answered, "but you can count on this, while I am in good health I'll not flee before the three of you. I advise you to give up those charges which you have brought against the girl. She has assured me upon her word of honor that she has never done offense to her lady nor betrayed her, and I shall defend her cause as long as I am able."

"Your death is now prepared, if you so choose," they answered, "but see to it that your lion does not do us harm."

"I did not bring this lion here for the purpose of having it be a berserker or fight a duel," replied Íven, "and I do not ask for any better assistance than I myself can provide. But if it happens that the lion rushes upon you, then defend yourselves against it, for I do not intend to answer for its acts."

"Unless you chastise your animal," they said, "then be on your way, because you will have nothing more to do here. Throughout the whole district everybody knows how the girl betrayed her lady. It would be most fitting for her to receive flame and fire for her betrayal."

"May the Holy Ghost never permit you to accomplish that," said Íven, "for I know the whole truth in this case. May God not let me leave here before I have rescued her." Then he said to the lion, "Leave us and lie quietly." The lion did as he said.

Next all three charged at him at once. Íven rode toward them leisurely, for he did not wish to meet them impetuously at first. They broke their lances on him, splintering them on his shield, while he kept his whole. Then he suddenly raced his horse away from them, but immediately charged back as fast as he could. He met the steward, who was foremost of them, and knocked him off his horse. That one was so badly off from the lance thrust that he lay there unconscious for a long time. The other two, drawing their swords, now rode at Íven and struck great blows at him, but they received even greater ones in return. There was a fierce exchange, but Íven defended himself so well against the two that they were unable to do anything to him. Then the steward got up and did as much harm as he could. When the lion saw that they were dealing its master such great blows, it did not intend to delay helping him any longer, for it was clear that he needed its assistance then. All the women who were near them prayed to God that Sir Íven would not be defeated. Then the lion came up and immediately attacked the steward, who was now on his feet, so that the rings of his mail flew off as if they were bran. The lion pulled at him with such force that all his flesh and skin came off down from the shoulder to the side. All his bowels were exposed. The lion rushed at once at the others. It did not want to withdraw, in spite of the blows and threats from its master who was trying with all his might to stop it and drive it back. None the less it rushed at them fiercely so that they complained greatly of its attack. The two dealt the lion great wounds and tired it out. Íven's heart was very distressed at this, and, becoming enraged, he hastened to avenge it with all his might. He attacked the two so fiercely that they could neither defend themselves against him nor withstand his blows. They finally surrendered themselves into his power because of the assistance given him by the lion which was by then so badly wounded that Íven was distressed by its injuries. Sir Íven was also badly wounded, but that seemed to him nothing in comparison with the animal's wounds.

Now Sir Íven had realized another of his intentions: now the young lady had been rescued from death and was completely reconciled with her lady. Later, those who had condemned the girl were burned at the stake, according to the judgment. The girl Luneta was free now and happy that her lady was reconciled and at peace with her. The people offered Sir Íven their hospitality and service, as was fitting, but they did not recognize him, nor did his lady, for he had concealed his mind and heart. Still, the lady made many entreaties, asking him if it were not his desire to remain with them for as long as he wanted and to seek recovery for himself and his lion.

"It is not possible for me to remain here even for a day," said Íven, "until that lady who is angry with me forgives me her ill will."

"God knows," the lady replied, "I am very displeased that you are unwilling to stay here with me, and I would not call that lady courteous who is angry with you. It never befits a good woman to shut her gate to such a good knight as you, unless he wronged her greatly."

"My lady," Íven said, "our dealings are now at a close. Whatever the reasons for my action may be, I do not wish to discuss them with anyone, unless they are familiar with the situation already."

"Doesn't anyone know the cause except you and your lady?" she asked.

"My lady," he replied, "you are the third."[14]

"Tell me about it, my lord," she said, "and then depart a free man."

"That will not be the case with me," declared Íven, "because I have more to make up for than I could ever bring about. It is fitting, as it happens, to conceal the matter no less from you than from others. However, I am called Knight of the Lion."

"What is the significance, my lord," she asked, "of your wanting to be called thus? We have neither seen you nor heard you mentioned before."

"From that you can decide that I am not a famous man."

"My lord," she said, "if you would not be displeased, I would like to ask you again to stay here."

"I would not remain, unless I were certain that I was once again reconciled with my lady."

"Good sir," she said, "may God grant that you fare well, and may He turn your sorrow and grief into consolation and joy—for peace and freedom, for happiness and a pleasant life."

"May God hear your words," Íven replied and then added softly under his breath, "obtain for yourself the key to the chest, for you are the lock, and I the key. Without knowing it, you are my consolation."

CHAPTER 13

Sir Íven left then and met no one who recognized him, except Luneta. She accompanied him on the way for some distance. He asked her not to reveal who it was had fought alone against three to rescue her from death. "My lord," she said, "that shall never be revealed by words of mine."

With fair speech he also asked her to remember him and when she found the occasion to reconcile him with his lady. Luneta replied that she would be happy to do that, and thus they parted.

Íven was now very worried about his animal's wounds and was concerned that it could not come with him. He made a bed of moss for it on his shield, placed the lion on it, and transported it thus until after some distance he came to the gateway of another stronghold, that of a great lord. The dwelling was provided with large, sturdily constructed quarters. Íven found that the gate was locked; so he called out, and it was opened for him at once. When he had entered the courtyard, he found a very large retinue there. Taking his horse and weapons, they all made him welcome. As soon as the lord of that mighty stronghold heard of Íven's arrival, he came into the courtyard to greet him. His lovely wife, as well as their sons and daughters, accompanied him, and they provided quarters for Íven and great hospitality.

Íven's wounds healed, as did those of the lion, and soon they were on their way. They went through woods and forests until they came to a large fortress. The name of this castle was "Encounter with Adventure."

As Íven rode toward the gate, some one shouted out: "Turn back, you ruffian! Do not ride through this gate or you will meet with a quick death tomorrow. Whoever directed you here did an evil thing."

"This is not a very nice way to receive a stranger," replied Íven, "I'll ride wherever I wish, in spite of you—come what may!"

Íven and the girl rode into the castle now.[15] On a level field they saw a good three hundred girls sitting, thin and poorly clothed, yet all extremely lovely. Some were weaving precious materials, some were weaving clothing, and some were spinning gold or silk. All were weeping and sorrowful. Íven rode up and asked what the cause of all that was.

One of the girls answered: "May God protect you, good knight, it would have been better if you had never come here. Many a knight before has tried to ride in here and free us from our misery, but all have met their death."

"Tell me, lady," said Íven, "what is the cause of your distress. I shall do what I can about it."

"I'll gladly tell you," the girl replied. "It so happened that a certain king named Reinion, of the kingdom of Hungary, rode to this place with his warriors. However, he was doomed to failure because of two accursed black sons of a giant who challenged him to a duel. He fought against them but was finally defeated. To ransom his life, he had to agree to send them three hundred of the loveliest and most courtly maidens as slaves. This situation was to continue until a knight came who could rescue us by surpassing the two and conquering them. But no such person has come yet. Ride now, my lord, to the master of the house, who is a short distance from here. There you will be well received, but tomorrow you will have to fight this duel, if you want to rescue us."

"I am certainly going to do that," Íven declared.

Íven then rode to the hall of the castle where there were many people gathered. No one, however, was so courteous as to take his horse or even greet him. He received nothing but mockery and scorn there. He rode on into a lovely garden where he found a mighty lord—who, he decided, must own the castle—along with his daughter, the loveliest of creatures. They, and all those who were in the garden, welcomed Íven with great friendliness. Their horses were taken at once, and they remained there enjoying the greatest hospitality during the night. The daughter of the house waited upon Íven.

In the morning Sir Íven asked the master of the house for leave to ride on his way.

"My lord," the master answered, "I would be glad to allow you to go your way, but I have no power to do so. There are two sons of a giant here against whom you will have to fight before you leave. They have dishonored and vanquished as many men as the number of those girls whom you saw yesterday evening, all of whom they have held in slavery here ever since. It is my wish, now, to give you my daughter, my castle, and all my kingdom, if you can conquer them."

"God forbid that I should bargain like that for your daughter," said Íven, "but rather, as far as I am concerned, she shall always be free."

"I see that you, in your faintheartedness, are rejecting my daughter," answered the master of the house, "but you're still going to have to fight, just the same."

At that moment the two accursed men appeared, big as giants and hideous in every respect. They had two clubs, completely studded with iron spikes, and two round bucklers. When the lion saw them, it began to roar and became angry with vexation. It curled itself up like a porcupine and beat the ground with its tail.

When the two saw the lion, they addressed Sir Íven: "Ruffian, take your lion away from this field and put it some place where it can't do us any harm. Then come onto the field and amuse yourself with us. However, if the lion is present, it will want to help you."

"I see that you are afraid of the lion," Íven replied, "but I would be delighted to see it attend to you a bit."

"It's perfectly obvious," they said, "that that's not the way it's going to be—you are going to do what you can, but all alone!"

"Where do you want me to put the lion?" Íven asked.

They showed him a little room and told him to lock the animal up there. It was done as they requested.

Sir Íven armed himself then and mounted his horse. The other two went at him with such great blows of their sledge hammers that his helmet, coat of mail, and shield were of little avail to him, for as soon as they struck his helmet, it

cracked and bent, and his shield broke. In the little room the
lion was distressed and sad now and wanted badly to get out.
It searched about carefully to see if there was any place it
could get out, because it heard the blows outside and thought
its master was in a bad spot. It kept trying hard and at last
found a crack under the sill. There it got out. By then Íven
was very tired, because he had taken so many great blows
from those devil's sons. He had been unable to wound them
in any way, because they had been too well instructed in
fencing, and their bucklers were so hard that no steel sword
could cut into them.

At that moment the lion rushed onto the battlefield and
attacked the one of them so fiercely that he fell to the ground
completely. He would never get up either, unless he quickly
got assistance. His companion rushed over to help him then,
defending himself against the lion. It had already torn the
arm off at the shoulder of the other one, who was now lying
under the lion. The companion had now become more
frightened of the lion than of its master and turned his back
on Sir Íven. When Íven saw that the other's neck was
exposed, he quickly cut at the neck so that the head flew off
and fell to the ground far away. He dismounted then to get
the one whom the lion was holding away from it. That one lay
as if dead, for he could not move in any way.

He could speak, however, and said: "Good master, take
your lion off me and don't let it rip me any more. Now you
can do whatever you want. But each person who requests
mercy has the right to obtain it—unless he meets a man who
has none. I can defend myself no longer. I give myself fully
into your power, so you need have no fear of me."

"Then the lion has made peace with you—if you *are* able to
live," answered Íven.

CHAPTER 14

After that, all the people came running up and
surrounded Sir Íven. The mighty lord and his wife received
him joyfully and asked him to be their lord and chieftain.

"This I request," Íven replied, "that you free for me all

those poor girls who have been tormented here."

"I'll do that happily," the lord said, "but would you, please, accept my daughter's hand, and I shall give you my whole kingdom as well."

"I can't accept your daughter," Íven answered, "for I am involved in some extraordinary circumstances because of that girl who is with me. I have promised to fight for her and save her case, if my life holds out."

The lord now offered Íven as much gold as he desired, but Íven refused it, took leave of the master of the house and his daughter, and rode out of the castle with the girl who had been accompanying him. All the maidens whom he had freed accompanied him out of the castle. They bowed to him, thanking him for their release, and bade him travel in God's care. All the people of the place begged his forgiveness for those foolish words they had spoken to him the evening before.

Then Íven rode with the girl until they came to the stronghold where King Arthur was holding court. The day had now come which had been appointed as the time for the girl to bring forward her champion. If such a knight did not come, the girl's sister would become the sole owner of all the property. That night Íven and the girl took quarters for themselves outside the stronghold, where no one recognized them. Already several days earlier Sir Gawain had ridden out of the stronghold, but on this day he returned with such weapons that no one recognized him. Usually he could always be recognized by his arms.

When noon had passed, the other girl, who had remained at court ever since the two sisters had parted, now declared that she wished to disinherit her sister. She addressed the king and his court: "Now I request, my lord, that you adjudge to me all the property which my father possessed. It is now obvious that my sister has been unable to find herself a champion, since the final day of our appointed meeting has now passed."

At that moment Sir Íven and the girl came riding up. He had shut the lion up in the house where they had spent the night. The king perceived that the girl had now come and had found a champion for her case.

She approached the king, greeted him, and said: "This courteous knight has accompanied me here to defend my case, even though he had enough serious business where he was, and may God bless him for that. Now I ask *you*, my sister, to give me my property. I do not wish to have one penny of your share, and I trust that good knights will not have to fight each other on our account."

But the younger sister replied: "I'd rather be burned in a fire than give you any assistance."

They ceased their quarreling at that, and each led her knight forward. All the people now rushed up to see the battle. This was a strange situation here, for those two men were to fight with deadly hatred who would normally each be willing to give his life for the other. But now they were deadly enemies, each wishing to destroy the other.

CHAPTER 15

Now the two knights rode at each other. When they came together, the stout lances they were holding both broke. Neither said a word to the other. They immediately drew their swords and struck at each other in so violent an attack that no one had ever seen such a duel by two men. The crashes from their blows were so great that when steel met steel it could be heard for four miles around. Their shields were badly cut then, their helmets broke, and their coats of mail split. Both were wounded and tired, and they finally had to dismount from their horses. The people were saying that those sisters ought to be reconciled, and the older one should get a third or a quarter of the property. But the younger one wanted no such thing, because she believed she had found the knight whom no one in the whole world could match. She was both foolish and malicious.

Hearing all this, the two knights jumped on their horses and fought twice as fiercely as before. It seemed strange to everyone that the two were so evenly matched. They had been fighting for so long now that the day began to turn into evening and the light dimmed. They were so tired by then that their arms could no longer raise their swords. It was so hot that the blood boiled in their wounds. Neither desired to fight any longer, because darkness was coming on them. Each now feared the other greatly, for their helmets were cut away completely. They both stopped.

Then the courteous Íven said: "Sir Knight, I believe that no one can reproach us now, because night has separated us. For my part, I wish to declare that you are worthy of great praise. Never in my life have I had such a battle or felt such pain. Never did I think I would meet the knight who could deal me so many great blows."

"God knows," replied Sir Gawain, "that you are probably not as distressed or tired from my blows as I am—and more—from yours."

"I think," said Íven, "if I knew who you really are, I would be very distressed."

"If you have been struck by any of my blows," declared Gawain, "then you have paid it back well. Now I'll not conceal my name from you—I am Gawain, son of King Loth."

When Sir Íven heard this, he began to shake all over with sorrow, and he hurled the bloody sword he was holding far away on the field. His shield, which was already split, he broke completely to pieces and immediately dismounted.

"Lord God," he cried, "what a sorry lack of recognition and what a great misfortune that we two should not have recognized each other sooner! If I had only known, I would never have borne weapons against you. Instead, right at the very beginning I would have given myself up as vanquished on the field of battle. For I am Íven, who loves you above all living men. Wherever I have been, you have always, in all matters, exalted, esteemed, and honored me far above yourself. Now because I have wronged you, even though unwittingly, I desire to surrender myself, vanquished, into your power. I am so wounded and tired that I can no longer fight."

"But I am completely overcome by your mighty blows," Gawain answered, "and I don't say that just to praise you. Even if you were quite unknown to me, I would give myself into your power rather than exchange any more blows with you."

At this they embraced, and each declared himself vanquished by the other. When the king and his court saw this, they came over and wanted to know what the cause of this rejoicing was—after such a long battle and so much distress. The king asked who they were and what the reason for their joy was.

Sir Gawain answered: "I am Gawain, your nephew. In this battle I did not recognize my comrade Íven—who stands here before you now—until he asked my name and we then told each other who we were. If we had fought any longer, he would surely have slain me. I would have been acting unfittingly, since I was pursuing an unjust cause."

Then Sir Íven spoke: "Good sir and dearest friend, I am right in venturing to tell my lord the king and his men that I have indeed been attacked and vanquished in this battle by Sir Gawain."

This exchange lasted a long time with each attributing the victory to the other. After listening to this, the king spoke: "In as much as each of you attributes the victory to the other one, I am willing to serve as judge of you two, as of all of you."

They placed the judgment in the hands of the king and then rode back to their quarters, where their battle dress was removed. At that moment the lion came running up, and the people became very frightened. Íven told them not to be afraid—"this is my companion, and I'll guarantee for it."

The lion rushed to Íven and greeted him in its own fashion. Now Gawain realized that this was the man who was known as the Knight of the Lion, who had won great renown and rescued his sister's children. "So I have wronged you in every respect," said Gawain, "and for that I ask you to forgive me."

After that the best doctors were found and their wounds were bandaged. When Íven and Gawain were both quite recovered and fit, the king pronounced the settlement. First, Sir Gawain and Sir Íven were to be brothers, just as they had been before. Then, the girls were to divide equally everything they had inherited from their father. Íven and Gawain were also to be declared equals in knighthood throughout the world ever after.

CHAPTER 16

When Sir Íven had been at the king's court for a long while there came over him that same sorrow which he had suffered before for his lady. He again thought about leaving the court secretly and riding to the spring. There he would raise a great din and a storm so that his lady would have to become reconciled with him—"or else I'll never stop causing the lightning to flash at the spring." So he left the court of the king without any one being aware of it.

Íven's lion went with him, because as long as the knight lived, it did not want to give up his companionship. They went on until they came to the spring, and Íven caused the lightning to flash so much that all the people who were in the stronghold with his lady were afraid, thinking the place would come crashing down. They wished that they were in Persia rather than here within these walls which shook so much. They were so terrified for their lives that they cursed their forefathers, saying: "Woe be unto them who first established their abode and built their houses in this district. In the whole world there is no place more fitting for people to hate than this one—where one lone man can torment us and make us tremble so."

Then Luneta spoke out: "My lady, it is fitting now that you seek for and be given good advice. You won't find anyone who could aid you in this difficulty unless you search far off. You have no one in your kingdom who would have the courage to defend the spring and uphold your honor."

"It's certainly useless to consider anyone who is here now," the lady replied, "but since you are wise, give me some good advice. When you're in trouble, you should have recourse to a friend."

"God grant," said Luneta, "that we might find the valiant knight who killed the giant and singlehanded vanquished three others—the one the lion follows. If you were to reconcile him with his lady—he is out of favor with her, but he loves her more than life itself—and if he were here, he would rescue you and your kingdom."

"I beg you to go in search of him," the lady answered sorrowfully, "and I promise you that I shall make good everything you have just said."

"My lady, do not be angry with me for what I am going to say," said the girl, "but I wish to have these promises of yours confirmed, so I won't be telling him a lie. I would like to hear your oath on the matter."

"I'll do that gladly," the lady replied.

Luneta now took sacred relics and gave them to her lady, saying: "I don't want you to lay charges against me tomorrow that you swore the oath because of me, but rather because of your own needs."

After that she prescribed an oath to her lady to the effect that the knight who was accompanied by a lion was to be reconciled with his lady—each with the other, as when they had been on the very best terms.

When the oath had been sworn, a gentle palfrey was saddled, and Luneta mounted at once and rode to the spring. She found Sir Íven and his lion there and, dismounting, welcomed him joyfully: "I'm happier at finding you now than I've ever been since I was born—except when I saw you riding toward the stake. I've obtained an oath from my mistress that she shall again be your lady, and you her lord."

Hearing this, Íven became exceedingly happy: he had never thought he would hear this. "I am afraid that I'll never be able to reward you for your kindness and service," he said and kissed her many times.

"You have been deserving of this service from me for a long time," she replied.

Then they mounted their horses and rode to the castle. The lady was delighted when she heard that the girl had returned and brought with her the knight who was accompanied by a lion. She was very eager to see him. Seeing her, Íven, in full armor, threw himself at her feet, while Luneta stood there and said: "My lady, respect your oath now and reconcile him with his lady. You alone can accomplish that."

The lady stretched out her hand, raised him up, and said that she would do everything she could to see him redressed.

"God knows," Luneta said, "his case is entirely dependent on

your will and power. And you'll never find a better man than
he. God grant that you both enjoy a love and affection so
steadfast that it never will disappear as long as you both shall
live. Give up your anger now and forgive him, my lady, for he
has no other lady than you. This is truly Sir Íven, your
husband."

At that the lady jumped up—"You have deceived and be-
trayed me with your evil tricks. You have tried to force me to
love someone who has never loved me and thinks nothing of
me. You have acted wretchedly and ill served me. I'd rather
waste all the rest of my life dealing with the water and wind,
the lightning and the foul weather. If it didn't mean slander,
reproach, and sin for me to swear false oaths, he would never
get any reconciliation or consent from me, or any peace or
welcome, no matter what he might do. The sorrow he caused
me with his treachery, lies, and falsehood still burdens my
heart. But no matter how much I dislike it—there is no need
to go into that in detail now, since I am forced to be re-
conciled with him and consent to him."

When he heard this, Íven said: "My lady, my misdeeds beg
forgiveness for themselves. I have paid dearly for my folly
and lack of wisdom. For that reason I admit my guilt and
place myself in your power. If you are willing to receive me
now, I shall never wrong you again."

"Gladly will I receive you," answered the lady, "for I do not
wish to break my oath. I am now willing to make an agree-
ment between the two of us and establish a reconciliation
which can be relied upon, an inviolable peace and a wonder-
ful joy."

"I know without doubt," said Sir Íven, "that nothing in the
world will make me happier."

Sir Íven has now found the happiness which he so long
desired. So every one can be certain that never before in his
life has he been so happy. He has now brought his endeavors
to a happy conclusion, for he loves a lady, and she now loves
him. He can now forget all the trials and tribulations because
of the great joy which comes to him from his sweetheart.

Here ends the saga of Sir Íven, which King Hákon the Old
had translated from French to Norse.

1. The names and order of appearance of the wedding guests in the two main manuscripts of the saga do not agree with those listed in the various manuscripts of *Erec et Enide*. The saga does, however, adapt some of the lengthier descriptions and thus the following individuals can be identified: the saga's King Balldvin corresponds to the French Kerrins, the old king of Riel; King Sartinus is King Bans of Gomeret; Erbilis, the king of the dwarfs, corresponds to Bilis; Earl Masade from Vera is Maheloas of the isle of Voirre.

2. Reference to the belief that some people were "shape-changers," i.e., they had the ability to change into animals; cf. Introduction, p. xiii.

3. Reference to Nureddin (1118–74), ruler of Syria and predecessor of Saladin.

4. The eve of Saint John's Day, i.e., June 23.

5. Reference to the old belief that the wounds of a murdered person would bleed in the presence of the murderer.

6. The reference seems to be to the coming of King Arthur in a week.

7. Both Stockholm 6 and AM 489 omit any mention of the girl's return; in Stockholm 46 she does not leave in the first place.

8. "Sodal the Red"; Chrétien has *Esclados le ros* (1. 1970). We use the form in Stockholm 6 as being closer to the French; AM 489 has *Nadis*, while Stockholm 46 omits the name completely.

9. Here Stockholm 6 implies that the whole affair was not Íven's fault; AM 489 has "and if I transgressed against him."

10. As a sign of pledging their mutual faith; Chrétien states this clearly (11. 2066–68).

11. The text is not entirely clear here; apparently the thought is: if I were to keep this horse which I have taken from one of your knights, it would reflect on your honor.

12. There seems to have been a misunderstanding of the French here; mention of the "sister of the earl" (from Stockholm 6) makes little sense and finds no basis in the French. AM 489 refers to an "Earl Sestor," which may indicate a misunderstanding of Chrétien who says that Arthur was holding court at *Cestre*, i.e., Chester (1. 2680); Stockholm 46 has nothing corresponding.

13. That is, "Mountain-Harfir." Chrétien has *Harpins de la Montaingne* (1. 3857).

14. Íven's answer seems startling, and the lady somewhat dense for not following it up. It differs somewhat from the French where he merely answers "Yes, my lady," without expanding on it any (1. 4606).

15. No preserved text explains how Íven met the girl who now appears to be accompanying him; cf. Introduction, p. xvi.

INDEX OF NAMES

The index, in addition to its most obvious purpose of providing a list of the names (persons and places) which occur in the two sagas, is designed to furnish the corresponding French forms as found in Foerster's editions of Chrétien. The latter form in each entry follows the dash; if none appears, this indicates that a corresponding name does not occur in Chrétien's work. In the few instances where we use the common English form rather than the Old Norse, the latter is given in parentheses. We have omitted from the index the names of the wedding guests in *Erex saga* (chapter 6), since they—and the order of their appearance in the saga—do not agree with Chrétien, and the two primary manuscripts of the saga do not themselves mutually agree (see note 1 to the translation). These names, in any event, appear right together and can be located easily by anyone who wishes to consult them. Page references for *Erex* and *Íven* are not given, since they occur on almost every page of their respective sagas.